The Tracy Log Book
1855

The Diary of Charles Tracy on Mount Desert Island

First edition published June 1997.

Printed in the United States of America
10 9 8 7 6 5 4 3 2 1

TM

ACADIA PUBLISHING COMPANY
Bar Harbor, Maine

Bar Harbor, Maine

October 2003

The Tracy Log Book
1855
A Month in Summer

With original sketches and drawings by

Frederic Edwin Church

by permission of Anne Sidamon-Eristoff

Edited by Anne Mazlish

Under the auspices of the Mount Desert Island Historical Society

This book is dedicated to the memory of

Mabel Morgan Satterlee Ingalls

(1901 - 1993)

who would have been pleased to see the journal of her great-grandfather's first visit to Mount Desert Island in print and available to all who love the Island.

Table of Contents

List of Illustrations

[1]Provided courtesy of New York State Office of Parks, Recreation and Historic Preservation - Olana State Historic Site

[2]Provided courtesy of Southwest Harbor Public Library

[3]Provided courtesy of Mount Desert Island Historical Society

[4]Reprinted from *Lost Bar Harbor*, Down East Books

[5]Provided courtesy of Raymond Strout, Ahlblad Frame Shop

[6]Provided courtesy of Anne Sidamon-Eristoff

[7]Reprinted from *J. Pierpont Morgan...* The Macmillan Co., 1939 edition

[8]Provided courtesy of The Harvard Club of New York

[9]Provided courtesy of the Episcopal Divinity School, Cambridge, MA

[10]Reprinted from *Fidelis of the Cross...* G. P. Putnam's Sons, 1926 edition

AUSPICES

The Log Book is published under the auspices of The Mount Desert Island Historical Society, whose mission is to preserve its historic landscapes and the record of its people — resident and visitor, winter and summer.

The tidal wave of visitors from the Eastern Establishment that began in the mid-nineteenth century contributed, in a very particular way, to the uniqueness of Mount Desert Island among Maine communities. Recognizing the special beauty of the Island, where all the salient features of New England are gathered in a small area, they would use their great wealth and influence to create Acadia National Park. In the long run, their vision would dominate the Island's economy and irrevocably alter its social structure.

All this was perceived for the better by preservationists and with ambivalence by native settlers. The result for historical record keeping is a rich complexity of life on the Island, and a creative tension underlying choices for the future and its growth.

PROSPECT = VIEW OR OVERLOOK

TRAMP = WALK OR HIKE

Sponsors

The limited hardcover printing of the Tracy *Log Book* was made possible by a small sponsoring group of summer visitors, many of whom have ties to Mount Desert Island that go back a number of years. To each of them, the Mount Desert Island Historical Society wishes to express its profound gratitude for recognizing the significance of the diary in the Island's historical record, and for their generosity.

The Society thanks Mrs. Gordon Gray, Mrs. Gerrish H. Milliken, Mr. Peter Blanchard, Mr. and Mrs. Daniel Pierce, Mrs. Vincent Astor, Mr. and Mrs. Gilbert Butler, Mr. and Mrs. Curtis Blake, Mr. and Mrs. Peter Iselin, Mr. and Mrs. Fitzgerald S. Hudson, Mr. Thomas A. Cox, Dr. Edward K. Dunham, Mrs. Nancy Harris, Mrs. Emily M. Beck, Mr. George Cheston, Mr. and Mrs. Alan Stone, Mrs. Gertrude McCue, Mrs. Richard Cobb, Mr. and Mrs. William Foulke, Sr., Mrs. Susan Mary Alsop, Mrs. Edward Spingarn.

Acknowledgements

We have many people to thank for the evolution of *The Log Book* into this publication.

Foremost, we wish to thank The Pierpont Morgan Library for access to the original journal which was deposited there by J.P. Morgan, Jr., the grandson of its author, Charles Tracy. In particular, we appreciated the encouragement and help of The Morgan's Director, Charles Pierce, and the many considerate members of the library's staff.

We are particularly grateful to Anne Eristoff, great-granddaughter of Charles Tracy, who made available to us for publication nineteen original Frederic Church sketches dating to the time of the diary visit (see pages 81-109), and two original drawings (see pages 47 and 111) by Church dedicated to two daughters of Charles Tracy, Annie and Frances, the latter who became the wife of J. Pierpont Morgan. These sketches and drawings were not in any collection of Church's work, or known previously to scholars of his work. We also have Miss Eristoff to thank for a visit to the Charles Tracy homestead on the Hudson River, and for providing us with family history, genealogy, and photographs of Tracy family members that appear in this volume. Her contribution has made this book a unique collection of materials.

In addition, there are many others who have contributed their thoughts, help and advice while we researched various aspects of the journal and identified individuals mentioned in the journal. Richard Allen, Vice-President of the Historical Society, deserves credit for first suggesting that we look into the original manuscript to see what it would yield. Nancy Howland of Jesup Memorial Library in Bar Harbor made our task ever so much easier by allowing us to photocopy a much-edited transcript of the original to work with in The Morgan Library. We are indebted to Dorren Martin and James Ryan, Director of Olana State Historic Site, for showing us the original Church drawings of Mount Desert in their collection, for a tour of Church's house, and for many good suggestions as well as help with research on several members of the Tracy party. The Cooper Hewitt Museum in New York City also contributed greatly to our initial research on Church's work on Mount Desert Island. We also owe sincere thanks to Constantine Eristoff, brother of Anne Eristoff, for his support and interest in the project from the start, and his cooperation at a key juncture in the reproduction of Church's drawings.

Other institutions and individuals who aided in the complex process of background research and the identification of members of the party were: The Library of Congress, Jesup Memorial Library, Brookline Public Library, Harvard University Reference, Boston Public Library Art Department, Julie Russell at Southwest Harbor Library, Steve Kuehler and David Siegenthaler of the Episcopal Divinity School, The Episcopal Diocese of Boston, the Rev. George Chapman of St. Paul's Church of Brookline, New York Historical Society, the New York Public Library, and Mary Saunders of the Harvard Club of New York. Also, Sandra van Heerden, Charles Jones, Anne Wyman, Gertrude McCue, Nancy Allen, Raymond Strout of Ahlblad's Frame Shop, John Baer, Charles Warner, Alexander Goriansky, Ralph Stanley, Meredith Hutchins, Geraldine Sweet, Nan Lincoln of the Bar Harbor Times, Kathleen Miller, Marianne and Wade Hancock, Peter Bachrach, Sally Merchant of the Mount Desert Town Office, and The Rockweed Society, all made important contributions. Thanks to Jaylene Roths, Director of the Mount Desert Island Historical Society, for her help and for shouldering some extra burdens during the final preparation of this manuscript. And, of course, thanks go to Frank Matter and Julie Savage of Acadia Publishing Co. for all their work and advice.

A constant and invaluable reference for our research on Frederic Church's sketches and drawings was Gerald Carr's two-volumes of the *Catalog Raisonné of Works of Art at Olana State Historic Site*, Cambridge University Press, 1994.

A.M.

Preface

I was delighted when I was informed by Anne Mazlish that she wished to edit and publish *The Log Book* of Charles Tracy for the benefit of the Mount Desert Island Historical Society. The autographed manuscript of this diary was in the Archives of The Pierpont Morgan Library, having been given to the Library in 1932 by J.P. Morgan, Jr., the grandson of its author. I was especially interested in her project because I knew that this diary had never been published before and because I learned that one of the travellers on this trip to Mount Desert in 1855 was Frederic Edwin Church. Here, then, was a remarkable document from the middle of the nineteenth century, which provided a vivid and charming account of a month spent on one of the most beautiful islands in the world. That it was an island that five generations of my own family had known and loved made its publication even more appealing. I am confident that this diary will give pleasure both to the visitor who has just discovered this island where the mountains reach into the sea and to those of us who have known its rocks and rills for as long as we can remember.

Charles E. Pierce, Jr.
Director, The Pierpont Morgan Library
New York City

March 4, 1997

Foreword

"A thousand good things come in every day, which ought to go upon the Log Book..."

— CHARLES TRACY, August 6, 1855

The Log Book is a delightful day-to-day account of a month long* visit to Mount Desert Island in 1855. From the first moments of the family's departure from New York City, the diary conveys the charged anticipation of travel and adventure. Written by Charles Tracy, a prominent New York lawyer, *The Log Book* is one of the earliest and more complete accounts of Mount Desert Island in the mid-nineteenth century, shedding light on the times and customs of summer visitor and native alike. Tracy's graceful narrative will strike a familiar chord in every reader who has "discovered" Mount Desert Island and made it his own.

In all likelihood, it was Frederic Edwin Church, a painter of the Hudson River School, who instigated the trip. He was already a recognized artist who initially came to the Island in 1850. No doubt, he first heard about Mount Desert from his teacher, Thomas Cole, who had been here earlier in the 1840s. Church was one of Tracy's large party of visitors, numbering twenty-seven and including whole families: parents, children and nurses. The gentlemen were socially and professionally influential members of the East Coast Establishment, which, at its peak in the nineteenth century, was a network of individuals from a similar

---

* Including arrival and departure, thirty-seven days precisely. The diary also contains a concluding account about Mount Desert Island.

cultural background, clustered around the great urban centers from Boston to Philadelphia.

The journey was an ambitious undertaking, involving three days and two nights of marathon travel by coach, steamboat, train, wagon and sailboat. The majority of the large party was tucked into the Mount Desert House in Somesville for the entire month of August. The visitors roamed the length and breadth of the island; climbing its mountains, picnicking on the shores of its lakes and ponds, rowing, sailing the Sound, hunting, fishing, visiting its native families, and merry making in the evening with music, dancing and games — much as visitors still do today.

These travelers were not the first prominent summer visitors to Mount Desert, although theirs was the largest recorded group up to that time to come together and seek shelter in one village. It would seem that the group was but a part, even then, of a steady stream of wealthy and well-informed "adventurers" to an already well-trod "wilderness." The visitations began sometime around 1840, and the improved accessibility after this period, including regular steamboat service starting in the early 1850s, set in motion the great tide of tourists to come. From the diary account, one becomes aware of a constant traffic to and from the first port at Clark Point, Southwest Harbor, then part of the town of Tremont. We know that many distinguished artists preceded and followed Tracy's group of visitors; that Louis Agassiz, the great European naturalist and Harvard professor, made his way here in 1864.[1] One family in the diary, the Fay family, returned to Somesville again in 1867 with another party of friends. Only guest house accommodations were available in 1855, but by the 1870s and 1880s, hotels were blossoming everywhere, soon followed by the "cottages" built by tycoons of the Industrial Revolution.

Members of the Tracy party were in the prime of life in the summer of the diary visit — Frederic Church and Theodore Winthrop were youthful and vigorous bachelors in their late twenties, poised on the brink of success. The Tracys, the Fays, and the Stones were substantial families to begin with, already friends or soon to become friends, with fourteen high-spirited children who ranged in age from five to twenty. There were also five other unmarried young ladies, most in their twenties, in the party. Professionally, the men represented the law, the clergy, business, publishing, art and literature. As a group they had strong ties rooted in professional concerns, religious affiliations, educational background, social status, community leadership, and old wealth. This idyllic time in the lives of both parents and children would begin to disintegrate six years later with the start of the Civil War in 1861. By 1869, two of the young men would die in battle and for two of the young women, death would come from illness after childbirth. One young man would die and be buried in a distant sea; and one of the most promising of the young people present that wonderful summer would shatter the hopes and dreams of three families, by making a single decision in his own life.

~ ~ ~

The diary's existence has been known to a small number of people outside the Tracy family at least since the 1940s. All evidence points to George Dorr, the father of Acadia National Park, as having arranged to have it copied by his secretary, Phyllis Sylvia, and given to Jesup Memorial Library in Bar Harbor.[2] The original diary is at The Pierpont Morgan Library in New York City. It was donated to the Morgan Library in 1932 by J.P. Morgan, Jr., whose mother, Frances, was the daughter of Charles Tracy.

The copy made by Dorr/Sylvia was edited to suit the mores and sensitivities of the 1940s, and colored by some lingering Victorian attitudes. The changes included preferences of the day in punctuation and spelling. Some of these have been returned here to the original (including misspellings, quirky punctuation, or archaisms), others were left as corrected, or newly corrected for uniformity. Diaries tend to be written with the verve of the moment recollected, and with less regard for consistency in punctuation and grammar, or for being decipherable. Difficult though the handwriting may be, an authenticity or charm is lost when it is transcribed in print, in both Dorr's copy and this publication.

The passages excised from the original in Dorr's copy (and returned in full in this publication) are interesting in themselves and deserve some explanation. Today, the Dorr/Sylvia deletions would be called "political correctness." Specifically, they took from the original references to Catholic 'superstition' or other offensive remarks showing religious bias.[3] During the trip, Tracy turns for recreational reading to a serious work by a person named Lambruschini. With a little detective effort, it is discovered, in all probability, to be a book by Cardinal Luigi Lambruschini on the Immaculate Conception, or Virgin Birth, first published in English in 1855. The Immaculate Conception was proclaimed definitively by Pope Pius IX in late 1854, bringing to a close centuries-long argument within the Roman Catholic Church itself.[4]

However, in Protestant circles, the pronouncement was considered an outrage. At the time, bias against the Roman Catholic Church was common among Protestants in America, the dominant religious group, and the battle between Episcopalians and Catholics as to which church was the "true" church continued unabated.[5] (It is well to keep in mind that even the future philosopher Ralph Waldo Emerson, as a college student in 1823, was railing against "Roman superstition" and "...the common submission...of the Freedom of opinion to the ordinance of the councils and court of Rome."[6]) The Episcopal/Catholic battle for mind and heart continued as a theme throughout the lives of a number of the visitors, and later resulted in personal tragedy for at least one.

Charles Tracy was a deeply religious man, and so were his companions on the trip, Harrison Fay and the Rev. John Seeley Stone — all Episcopalians, members of the establishment church which looked to England for its heritage. It became clear in the diary that as long as the Rev. Stone remained with the party, both morning and evening devotions were observed, and Sunday honored. On at least two occasions, the party attended the Somesville Church (only erected in 1850), and Tracy comments on the service, the preacher, and those in attendance. It may startle readers to learn that Sunday church services in the mid-nineteenth century lasted four hours, with but a half-hour break for lunch. As an exception for the large party "from away" attending the local service, lunch was extended to a whole hour, limiting time in church to just three-and-a-half hours!

Not only does Tracy choose recreational reading on religious subjects, he engages in serious discussions about religion with the Rev. Stone.

Tracy's reverence for nature as God's handiwork is also powerfully felt and expressed. In truth, children of that era would not have found intense devotional concerns on the part of their elders at all unusual, and they would expect to share them. One of the party, Miss Fay, a member of the Rev. Stone's flock, in addition to providing regular evening entertainment at the piano, performs at all the group's devotions, with her brothers serving as choir. Not all in the party, however were quite so devout. We know that at least Frederic Church, who hailed from a stern Congregationalist family, espoused a more liberal variety of his family's faith.

Also excised from the original were most references to illness in the family, or personal discomfort. George Dorr, it should be noted, was a Bostonian, and in the mores and culture of New England, illness and complaint are things considered better kept to oneself. Not only good manners, but also proper self-effacement required this. But a diary is not polite conversation, and something is lost of the humanity of the diarist and the realities of his world when deletions are made.

Several poems were also dropped from the original text by Dorr/Sylvia. These poems of the nineteenth century upper class celebrated an occasion, or sentiment, showed literary accomplishment, and were *de rigeur* among the educated. While many of the well-born and well-educated professional classes were still writing 'occasional' poetry in 1855, it is well to remember that Walt Whitman and Emily Dickinson were then in the peak years of their creativity. As poetry, Dorr/Sylvia probably found most poems in the diary somewhat wanting by the 1940s.

Other passages omitted from Dorr's copy of the original include references to people as "oriental" (apparently Tracy's designation for something odd), perceptions of social rudeness, or personal references Dorr felt either too intimate or self-serving, any mention of alcohol, and other things deemed 'unnecessary' by Dorr/Sylvia. Dorr also wrote a six-page summary of the diary, in which he makes some interesting observations about the life and times in which the diary was written.[7]

Two controversial issues of the day, slavery and secession, also get a hearing in the diary, but are retained in Dorr's copy. There is more than a whiff of paternalism[8] in this section, even if subtly stated. Tracy, contemplating Daniel Webster's picture in Faneuil Hall while in Boston on the stopover during the journey to Maine, perceives the forces of agitation for "Negroe" liberation in the Northeast as a threat to the continuing Union of the States. He writes that he fears that it is the North that will secede! His anxieties for the future were fully justified when he lost a close friend from the summer party at the very start of the Civil War in 1861.

~ ~ ~

The journey to Somesville would be unthinkable today for a family of ten with very young children — the composition of Tracy's group alone. Prior to the steamboat, a journey overland from New York City might have lasted even longer, by at least a day and a night. However, compare the Tracy family's trip to Mount Desert with the return trips, pages 137 and 138 of the diary. By the time of the great influx of summer visitors in the 1880s and 1890s, steamboat service was more efficient and stops were made at all ports.

The reader may also note on the first page of the diary talk of the dusty streets of New York City, as the family proceeds by coach to the dock. Many of the city's major thoroughfares were still unpaved in that era, others were only brick or cobblestone.

Once in Somesville, the party either resorted to transport by wagon with slow plodding horses, or walked. In all accounts of the period, the wagons seem to break down quite frequently. The amount of walking in which individuals indulged startles readers today. Frederic Church, the painter, sets the tone for the group in this respect. He was forever jumping out of the wagon and sprinting ahead, getting home before the wagon arrived. Imagine regularly, without complaint, walking from Schooner Head to Agamont Park, Eagle Lake to Somesville, or Somesville to Southwest Harbor (then called the Town of Tremont) and back — this is exactly what was going on daily throughout the diary!

The diary contains much interesting information about the era in which it was writtten, some of which needs a little clarification; such as the journey down the "River," as Somes Sound was sometimes still called then (a hold-over from pioneer days), and the fact that Frederic Church had given Eagle Lake its name the previous summer. Lakes and ponds were pretty indiscriminately referred to as ponds in those days and many had no name beyond that of a directional one, such as Southwest Pond, or descriptive, such as Great Pond. The Tracy party took it upon themselves to name some of these ponds, such as Skating Pond (Round or Ripples Pond), Lily Pond (Somes Pond), Crescent Lake or Lake Silence (Great Long Pond), Loch Fay (Seal Cove Pond), Annie's Loch (perhaps Denning's Pond, now Echo Lake), Lake Notch (Upper Hadlock Pond), Twinhill Pond (Jordan Pond).

The reader becomes aware from descriptions of various excursions on the Island made by Tracy of how open the landscape was in 1855 compared to now. There was more farmland, and there were fewer mature trees and woods. The primeval forests were long since gone. If one looks at photographs of early summer cottages from the 1880s, one can see that the growth around them was scrubby, with less obstruction of views of ocean and rock. In the diary, when a wagon party sets off down the Seal Cove Road, Tracy notes that there is a high point from which they can see four lakes at once — probably what we now know as Great Long Pond, Round Pond, Hodgdon Pond and Seal Cove Pond — a view only possible from the air today.

From Eagle Lake, the summer visitors observed evidence of the Great Fire of 1835, which had swept over the western side of what they then called Newport Mountain, later Green Mountain, and now Cadillac. The name Newport mysteriously moved to what is now called Champlain Mountain overlooking Schooner Head, where the old Lynam farmhouse was located. Often mountains took their names from the men who lumbered them, such as Jordan and Sargent. The fire, it was said, burned for days, fed by a lumbered slash and a driving Southwest wind. The story still current in Dorr's account was that a small boy had set the fire, while guarding cattle grazing on the hardwood shoots of trees that had been cut for lumber. The boy confessed that he had set the fire because he wanted to see it burn! — a not unlikely possibility considering the long hours of boredom while tending a herd.

It is also interesting to note that the Coast Survey, a government department at that time, had a surveyor living on the top of Newport/Green/Cadillac Mountain for which purpose a road had been constructed. (Agassiz was often invited aboard the Survey's steamer to pursue his research on one of their coastal cruises.[9])

There is stark contrast between the comments of Dorr and Tracy on the naming of Mount Desert Island. Dorr states that the explorer Champlain "...named it on the spot L'Isle des Monts Déserts[10] — the island of the bare and lonely hills, a name that has persisted strangely through all change of race and times to the present day." Tracy says: "The better impression is that the French saw the mountains, looking like one grand mountain when approached from the east, and then missed it in the fogs, its form thus deserting them. They said it deserts us, and then named the mountains Mount Desert... If the New Englanders had named the place, the word Mount would be prolonged to Mountain and would be made to follow, not precede, the other term."

Although the party made its home base in Somesville, members of the group visited other popular guest houses as well, such as "the Roberts tavern," later known as the Agamont House (see page 41), opposite the present Agamont Park, and located in what was called East Eden (Bar Harbor). The Tobias Roberts' family was a prosperous one, and the two daughters, Irene and Iqua (unusual as those names may sound), [11] are mentioned in the diary when they were invited to the Tracy thank you/farewell party. Others of the party also made a number of excursions to the Lynam Farm on Schooner Head, a popular guest house (see page 43) located on a secluded cove near one of the more dramatic headlands of the island which is described in detail in the diary. Today, this area is all privately owned property, but it may be viewed from an overlook off the Park Loop Road. Clark Tavern (see page 35) in Southwest Harbor, which was alternately called The Island House, was another guest house.

The location of the guest house where the party stayed in Somesville is never named in the diary, but given the fairly detailed description (see page 37), it can be identified as the Mount Desert House (or Tavern), a building still intact today, with the same warren of rooms, particularly if present-day modern bathrooms are counted as bedrooms. The fact that the host is referred to as the customs officer is the strongest confirmation of this location. In all other accounts of the period his name is given as Daniel Somes, Jr., the proprietor of the Mount Desert House at that time. We also know there was a flagpole (mentioned in Tracy's account of their arrival) on the property, visible to us at least in the photographs of the 1880s. Virginia Somes Sanderson, in her history, *The Living Past*,[12] claims to have seen the party invitation to the Tavern, which the group sent out to the villagers at the end of their stay, and which again corroborates the location. Another corroborating account was made in a 1918 memoir by Adelma Somes Joy, who says they stayed at the "little tavern," but also suggests that some of the visitors were put up in other houses in the village.[13] Church, himself, sketched a view of the cove across the road from the Tavern (see page 39).

On the other hand, by Tracy's own account, the view from the main body of the house where the adults stayed — a view of the narrows, Bar Island, and Mason Point — suggests another inn in use as well. Only the Somes House Inn, across the road and managed by Daniel's cousin, George, seems to offer such a complete view. It is known that, at least eventually, either establishment could boast three houses, two for the visitors and one for the proprietor to fit the diary's description.

~ ~ ~

The full traveling party, when made up in Boston, consisted of twenty-six people from several families hailing from New York City, Brookline and Springfield, Massachusetts, and Hartford, Connecticut — ten Tracys, five Stones, eight Fays, and three Churches (included in the count were a Tracy nurse and a Fay nurse). It swelled to twenty-seven a few days later with the arrival of Theodore Winthrop. In the second half of August, some members of the original party departed and others replaced them keeping the number fairly constant.

Frederic Church made a record of events on the trip with sketches of members of the party engaged in some activity or another. Some of these sketches are comic and fanciful — nineteen of these have been discovered and are published in this book for the first time. Also, two little known drawings given as mementoes of the time to two of Tracy's daughters, Annie and Fan, are also published here (see pages 47 and 111). In addition, a number of portraits and photographs of the participants, close in age to the period of the visit, have been unearthed and are included in this publication, as well as pictures of the four guest houses visited.

Throughout the account, individual adult members of the party, including the young ladies, are referred to with their titles — Mr., Mrs. or Miss. Only the children are called by their first names. This was the custom of the time, even in an intimate account such as a diary. In the drawing room, the same formality would have prevailed in polite company. As a result, it took detective work to track down and identify the participants, many never fully named in the original account. Women were hardest to identify as they were often omitted from the historical record of that time. Wherever possible, information about who these people were, and what became of them, has been added in an Afterword. Many of the people who figure in the diary led lives which later took important, interesting, or tragic turns about which the reader might wish to know. The search for individual stories has been fascinating and suggestive. Some stories require more than an Afterword to do them justice.

The next few pages offer a cast list of the party which visited Somesville that summer of 1855. Names, ages, and professions (where known) are mentioned, as well as relationships among the individuals.

Anne Mazlish, Editor
Somesville

Members of the Party

— Biographical Information —

(Note: Further biographical information and what happened later in their lives appears in the **Afterword**.*)*

The Tracy Family

Charles Tracy — (1810 - 1885) father and diarist. At the time of the visit, Tracy was 45 years old and was a successful lawyer as well as socially prominent in New York City, where he and his family lived at 81 E. 17th Street. See portrait, page 145.

Louisa Kirkland Tracy — (1813 - 1885) his wife. See portrait, page 145.

Anne "Annie" Huntington Tracy — (1838 - 1864) age 17. Annie was the oldest of "the beautiful Tracy girls" as they were known in New York. See portrait, page 147.

Mary Kirkland Tracy — (1839 - 1882) age 16.

Frances "Fanny" or "Fan" Louisa Tracy — (1842 - 1924) age 13. She was the subject of two poems in the diary related to an incident on one of the party's mountain climbs, which caused much amusement. The diary reveals that she was a spirited young woman and a favorite of her father. See portrait, page 147.

Clara Tracy — (1843 - 1926) age 12.

Charles "Charlie" Edward Tracy — (1845 - 1896) age 10. Tracy's only son, Charlie often goes on outings with his father in the diary. See portrait, page 147.

Julia Noyes Tracy — (1850 - 1927) age 5. It is for Julia that a nurse was brought on the trip.

Cordelia Kirkland — age unknown. She was a niece of Louisa Kirkland Tracy, the daughter of Mrs. Tracy's brother, William. She is listed in an 1855 City Directory as living at 6 Lexington Avenue with her brother, Joseph Kirkland.

The Fay Family

Harrison Fay — (1806 - 1882) and his wife, **Sarah P. (Kelsey) Fay** (1808 - 1895). They lived at 43 Linden Place in Brookline, Massachusetts, a private enclave modeled after *Place Linden*, a showplace on the outskirts of Paris. There Mr. Fay and eleven other gentlemen built large distinctive homes in 1841. He was a wealthy Boston merchant. They had two daughters and three sons. Mr. Fay was active in the Episcopal Church, and a founder of St. Paul's Church in 1852, near his home and where his friend, the Rev. Stone, was the first rector. Most likely, he introduced both Stone, and another friend and neighbor, Robert S. Littell, to the party on Mount Desert Island. He was also an old friend of Charles Tracy.

Miss Cornelia "Cornie" Fay — (1835 - 1869) age 20. The musician in the diary, she was the organist at St. Paul's Church in Brookline. It was because of her skills that a piano was brought by boat from Boston to Mount Desert at the time of the diary visit. She regularly provided the music for the evening entertainment, and her brothers sang parts. Miss Fay's central musical role was again confirmed in a later diary account by Robert Amory when he accompanied the Fays on a return trip to Mount Desert and Somesville two years later. In a poem that she wrote to Theodore Winthrop after the 1855 trip, there is a suggestion of romantic interest between them at the time.

James "Jim" Harrison Fay — (1838 - 1920) age 17. See portrait, page 151.

Arthur Kelsey Fay — (1843 - 1869) age 12.

Clement Kelsey Fay — (1846 - 1898) age 9.

Frances "Fanny" Fay— (1849 - 1909) age 6.

The Church Family

Frederic Edwin Church — (1826 - 1900). At the time of the trip, he was age 29 and living in New York City. This was his fourth trip to Mount Desert. Already he was a recognized painter, having been elected to the National Academy of Art at age 23. Biographers describe him as tall, slender and high spirited. In the diary, evidence of his playfulness is seen in the sketches of "Two Hunters," the nineteen drawings included on pages 81-109. These sketches tell a mischevious story, depicting his friends, Mr. Tracy and Mr. Winthrop, on a hunting expedition, when actually they were just off for the afternoon on a mountain climb. Since the pair's luck at "shooting" to date was almost nil, in spite of Tracy's new gun, Church enjoyed a little humor at their expense. A quirk of his at the time, Church takes his own "siphon" coffeepot with him wherever he goes. See portrait, page 149.

The Sisters — **Elizabeth Mary** (1824 - 1886) age 31.
Charlotte Eliza (1832 - 1867) age 23.

Portraits at Olana State Historic Site, F.E. Church's former home, show them to be beautiful young women. At the time of the visit to Mount Desert Island, they still lived at their parent's home in Hartford, Connecticut.

* * *

Theodore Winthrop — (1828 - 1861) age 27 during the visit, he and Tracy were the resident poets of the party. Like his friend Church, he had dash and great vitality. He had already completed the "grand tour" of Europe obligatory for most wealthy young men in those days, as well as seven months of adventure out west, before he settled in New York to study law with Charles Tracy in 1854. See portrait, page 149.

The Stone Family

The Reverend John Seeley Stone — (1795 - 1882). The oldest known member of the party at 60 years. Described in all accounts (see Notes & Sources) as a handsome man of impressive height and carriage; a genial disposition, and largeness of spirit. It was said he also possessed an exasperating dose of absentmindedness. A leader of the Evangelical (low church) movement within the Episcopal Church, he was considered a leading orator of his day. (By contrast, the spiritual fare of the Somesville church would have been sterner and plainer, as well as Methodist/Congregationalist in doctrine). At the time of the visit to Mount Desert, he was rector of St. Paul's Church, Brookline (from 1852 to 1862) and a friend of the Fay family. He was accompanied on the visit to Mount Desert by his wife, and three of their sons. Three younger children had been left at home with whooping cough. This was a source of anxiety for the parents, who cut short their planned stay. See portrait, page 151.

Mary Kent Stone — (1807 - 1901) his wife, daughter of Chancellor James Kent of New York's Court of Chancery. Chancellor Kent was a famous jurist and author of *Kent's Commentaries*, an important treatise on American Law. His bust stands in the Library of Congress Reading Room. He also had a great influence on his grandson and namesake (directly below).

James Kent Stone — (1840 - 1921) called Kent, he was age 15 at the time of the Somesville adventure, and the oldest son of the Rev. and Mrs. Stone. He was also a close friend of James Fay, and he remains behind with the larger party after his parents and younger brothers leave. See portrait, page 151.

William "Willie" Stone — age unknown.

Henry "Hal" Van Dyke Stone — age unknown.

* * *

Robert S. Littell — age unknown. Also from Brookline, Mass., he was a friend of the Fay and Stone families and publisher at some point with his father, Eliakin, at Littell, Son and Co. The firm's best known publication was *Littell's Living Age*, a weekly, in which an article about Frederic Church's most famous work, *Heart of the Andes*, appeared in 1859, following the first exhibition of the picture. Eliakin Littell was a founder of St. Paul's Church with Harrison Fay. In one of Kent Stone's letters to his mother, he asks to be remembered to Robert Littell, suggesting the possibility of a friendship of peers, although his rowing adventure with Clara implies a greater maturity.

The Titus Family

Mr. George N. Titus and his two daughters, **Lucretia** and **Annie**, of 61 Irving Place, New York City and Springfield, Mass. Mrs. (L.A.) Titus is not mentioned. The Tituses appear to be friends of the Tracys to begin with, and after the trip, at least, become friends of the Church and Stone families with whom they may have again traveled, as suggested in correspondence between them. (Identification of this family needs further corroboration.)

Note: *Sources for the biographical information in this section are listed under* Notes and Sources *at the end of the book.*

Guest Houses and Scenes of Mount Desert Island

circa 1855

View of Mount Desert Island, sketch by Frederic Edwin Church, c. 1855-56

Clark's Tavern, also known as The Island House, in Southwest Harbor, Town of Tremont, c. 1880s

The Mount Desert Tavern, Village of Somesville, where the Tracy party stayed, c. 1850s

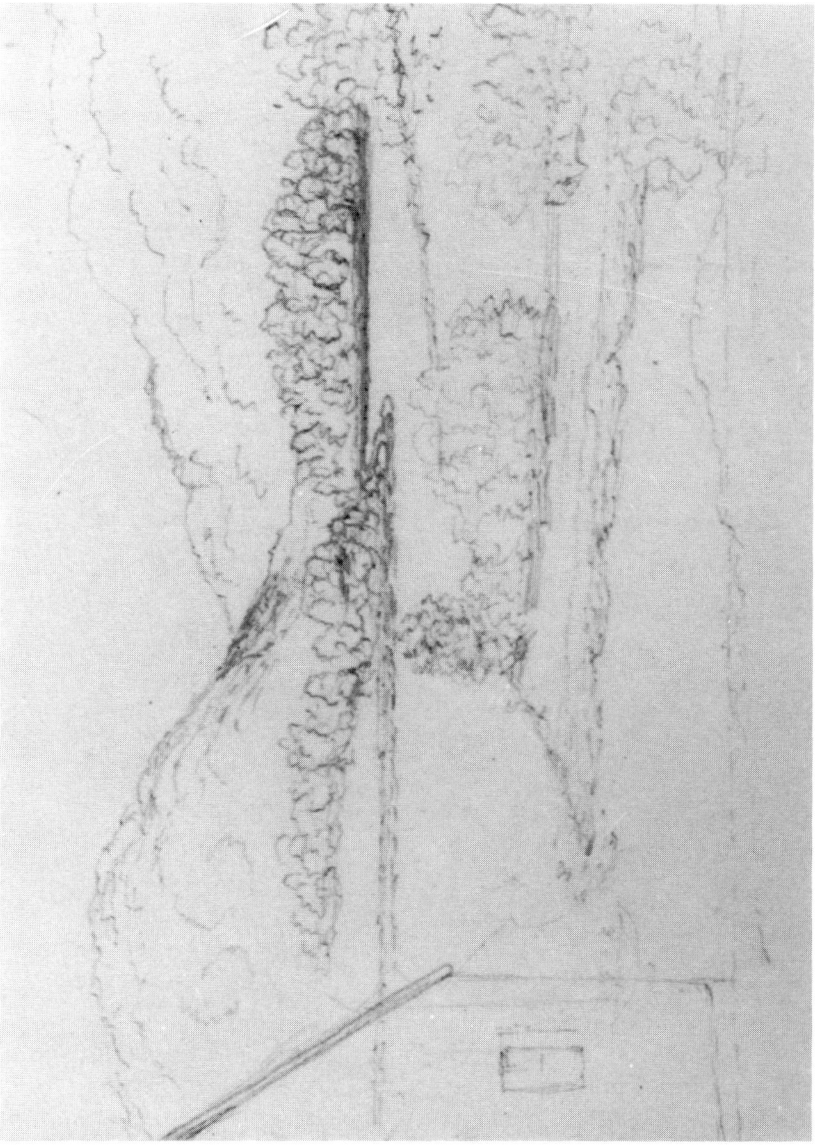

F. E. Church sketch from the Tavern of Somes Harbor, Meadow and Cove, and Whiting Store (now Port-in-a-Storm Bookstore), c. 1855-56

Roberts' Tavern, also known as the Agamont House, prior to 1888, East Eden.
It was opposite what is now Agamont Park in Bar Harbor.

Mr. George B. Dorr and Mrs. J. P. Morgan (Frances Tracy) at the Lynam Farmhouse near Schooner Head, c. early 1900s

Lumber Mill at Mount Desert Island, sketch by F. E. Church, c. 1850

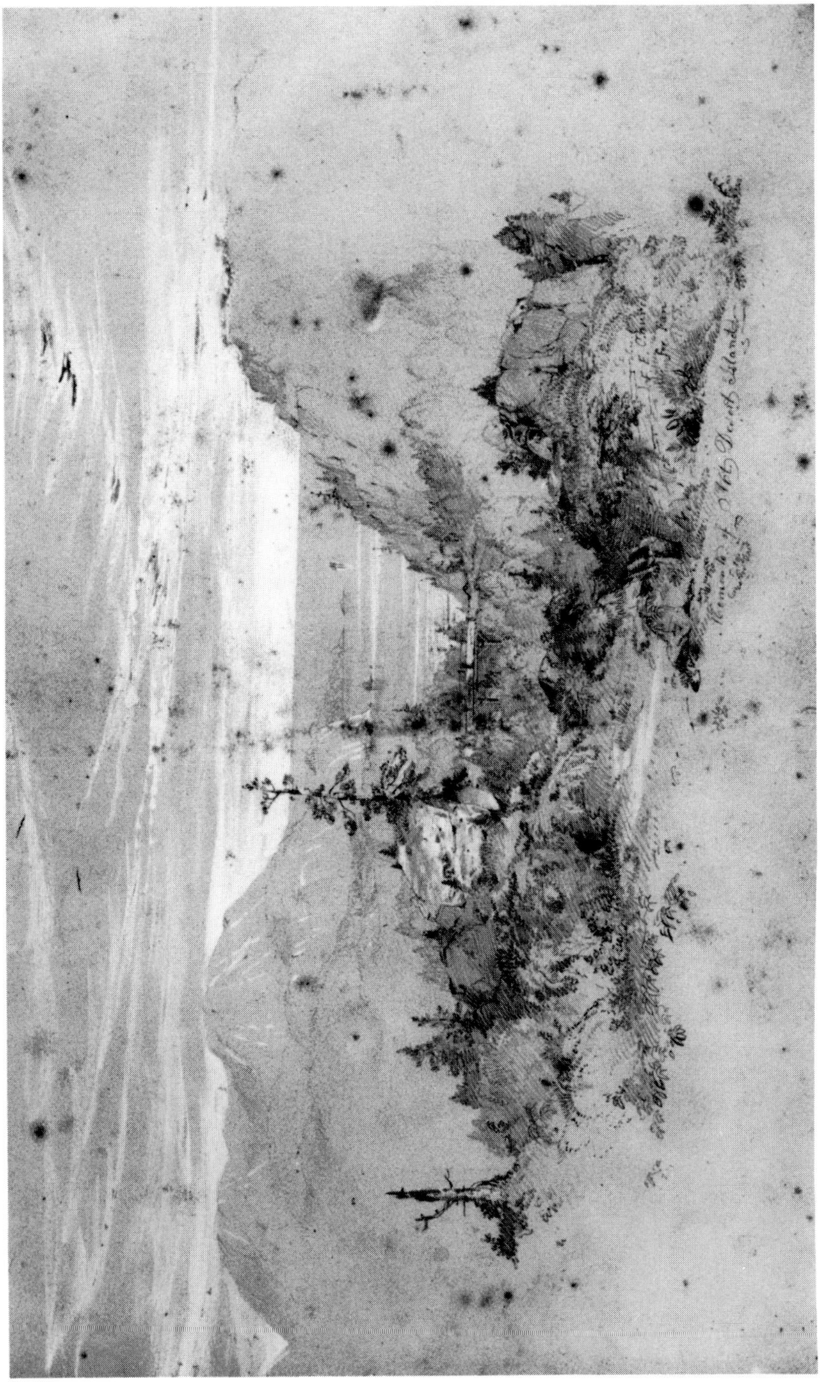

Inscribed ~ F. E. Church for Fan, 1855 Memento of Mt. Desert Island. [Tucked into the right hand rock is a woman in a long skirt and picture hat reading.]

THE LOG BOOK

Voyage
from New York to Mount Desert Island,
stay there, and return.
July - August - September, 1855

Written in most part by my grandfather Charles Tracy and given me by my mother, Frances Tracy Morgan, in the year 1916.*

— J.P. MORGAN

Given to The Pierpont Morgan Library
by Mr. J.P. Morgan, 1' March, 1932

*[The phrase "in most part" refers to the inclusion of poems by Theodore Winthrop. The day-to-day account is written entirely in Charles Tracy's hand.]

Monday. July 30. 1855. 81 E. 17th Street. N.Y.

At 3 1/2 p.m. the baggage is on the cart, and goes off - a good load of outfittings for a month on Mount Desert Island for a small family of ten. The children are absolutely ready! The hour for starting is future, but their "things" are present! Good omen!!

3h45m Great excitement on the premises, the coaches not being here on the instant.

3h46m Charlie dispatched to the stable to see what is the matter. He proceeds at full run, a few little voices piping after him, "quick:" "hurry."

3h50m Coaches drive up. All hands on the flagging.[1] Coachman pleads his watch and vouches for its time as true. Noted, a good excuse, but his watch clearly too slow.

3h50 1/4m C.T. and M.K.T. enter coach No. 1 and drive furiously to No. 6 Lexington Avenue.

4h precisely They return with Cordelia and her luggage; at 81 E 17th St. receive balance of load, and both coaches roll away, and down Broadway.

Watches are drawn at every block, and the progress is found sufficient to save the boat.

4 1/2 pm All hands on board the *Empire State*.

It was a cloudy day, almost raining at times. The ride was therefore comfortable, without heat or dust. The party thought kindly of Gotham; what a charming spot to leave in summer!

What a superb boat. Full one sixteenth of a mile long, with berths for a grand army. Such a load! More than all the seats would hold.

Nothing special happened at the embarkation excepting that the rubber bag containing certain robes de nuit, or nocturnal habiliments (anglicé nigh'gowns and nigh'caps) got into the crates & was locked up fast, to be unlocked at Boston. The ladies therefore expect to sleep standing.

At 5 we were off, and the staterooms all distributed and possessed.

Supper hour arrived, and it was of course impossible to muster 9 in time for the first rush; and so the courteous Steward ordered a second supper for our party and some of like condition. Appetites good, and victuals not bad, & consumption not small.

After supper we scattered over the boat. Fanny and I listened on the after deck to the voices of the boat and sea. We made them out at last. The engine murmured and groaned, the sea whispered, hush.

So hush travellers, and take your sleep.

Tuesday. July 31. 1855.

Point Judith[2] must have been off on our larboard, when this day began its first hour; for the boat rolled gracefully, and made a rocking cradle of all our berths. At daylight, we were in a fog, and the steam whistle brayed its donkey note, and the boat stopped and started, with a chorus of jerking bells. We peeped at Newport from our windows, and beheld a drowsy town, finishing its rest. Then up the river to Fall River,[3] smoking at a dozen high chimney-tops, and reminding us of the cottons which come out so white and fair from this cloud of smoke.

The Old Colony Rail Road took us next; in the steamboat train. We flew away, the cars went fast, and the party went fast asleep. Approaching Boston, the grand suburban land of villages dashed along under our windows, and we soon sailed through Quincy and by its quarries, and rushed into Boston.

A coachman between 6 and 7 feet high took us all into his "stage," and off we went, the horses actually galloping, to the Revere House.[4] Ablutions and breakfast followed; then Mr. Fay called, assuring us that we should meet him & his family on the boat at 5 pm.

In the morning the Churches arrived, and completed the party. Charlie and I went with the baggage to the boat, the *Penobscot*, at the end of Long Wharf, and coming back walked through Quincy Market, and paid our respects to Faneuil Hall. The grand motto of the Webster picture [5] - "Liberty and Union, now and forever" - ('one and inseparable' omitted, why?) struck me deeply as I sat in the old Cradle of Liberty. At this day, a set of enthusiastic and unquiet spirits have forgotten the prime truth at the bottom of this motto, that the union is essential to liberty. Noisily contending for the due liberation of three millions of negroes, they assail the union which defends the liberties of seven times three millions of caucasians, and which pledges the liberation of hundreds of millions more now under despotism. In this very hall these men come, and declaim against the Union itself; and the present movement in politics evidently looks to a political, if not governmental, division of the whole country into northern and southern.....I meant to leave business and public affairs to wag their own way for one month; but these thoughts have crowded upon me and I feel ugly.... and there is an end.

Boston Common is the head of Boston. The Frog Pond is the jewel in the brow of this green crest. The elms are its lovely and well barbered hair; and the grey squirrels are — are — the — jewelled & feathered adornment of the curls. A more lovely walk than the mall, is not; the double rows of elms present the type of gothic arches, and in one part present the true dropcenter of that style. Pity the common is not genteel!

Boston is a curiosity. Its crooked streets of variable width, its narrow lanes (called avenues), its courts, its superb market house, its long wharves, its ups and downs, its solid granite churches, its clean, old yellow State House, its antennae of bridges, its carts twenty five feet long, its tandem draught teams, its paper money printed like old continental, its old houses and its superb new ones, its clean streets, its "two and thrippence" worth three shillings, its beautiful harbor and bare islands, and (as you leave it) its shadow of Bunker Hill Monument, as it stands pointing to the skies, - all these are charming. So it was with the writing master whose copies ran —

"Many men are made saints on earth, who never reach — Boston."

At five p.m., just 24 hours since we left Pier 3, North River, the *Penobscot* took us from Long Wharf. The Fays and Stones had arrived and we now went forth, a party of 26...

The Sun took to the clouds; but some stars and the broad moon shone on us, after he was under water. The roll of the sea was very slight, but just enough to upset the ideas of several of the party. The little pocket flask of brandy was very useful, in some cases; but there are cases beyond medicine. It was a sight to see the ladies recumbent on mattresses in the saloon, raising their heads gently at times to embrace the basins, and the black chambermaid flying about, with a broad grin, feeling excited with that which prostrated the lands people. Some stood out & supped, and then succumbed, and some went through without overflowing. Mean while, a company of Orientals,[6] from "Maine State," grouped near the stern, sang chorus and glee through the whole range of negro music, and other people relieved themselves from the wound in the ear by gazing on the moons broad and long field of light in the sea as she rose above its horizon.[7] At eleven o'clock I found all of my family reposing, or at least quiet, & so ended my rounds.

Hoping for a sunrise from the sea, I roused several times, beginning at 3 o'clock; but it ended in a fog with a round of steam whistles, from the steamers near each other but invisible, and a foggy screen of the sun till some 7 o'clock.

Wednesday. Augt. 1. 1855.

The first clear air opened to us the coast of Maine, rough, broken, and wild. We sailed among islands to the region of the Penobscot river, & went aground about 20 feet from the dock at Rockland.

The baggage was mustered, and so were the passengers; and the little steamer *Rockland* [8] came alongside and took us all on board. We sailed across the Penobscot Bay, & between the Fox Islands, and along among the Cranberry Islands, soon seeing Mount Desert Island in the distance. A comfortable breakfast shortened the passage and by noon we were on shore at Tremont, the Southwest Harbor of the Island.

The Maine coast, during the 50 to 60 miles of this morning's sail, presented us a fine sight, including rocky mountains, bold shores, wide forests, and well cultivated farms. The number of small vessels, many of them laden with boards, was remarkable, and showed how much this coast is occupied with commerce in its own productions.

Mount Desert island appears at a great distance; at first, a pale line above the horizon, but gradually growing into a chain of hills, the most wild and picturesque, and as we drew in front of its south coast, the hills seemed to be divided and riven apart by deep cuts, going down to their foundations. Some were green with forests, & some were bald rock, hanging out abruptly over the water. Our party were intensely animated with the scene, and came on shore at Tremont in high spirits.

A dinner was served for us at the tavern there (Clark's),[9] cooked admirably, & containing in its catalogue of good things, fish chowder, clam chowder, ham, mutton, peas, new potatoes, pies, pudding, and French preserves, the latter being brandy peaches with a powerful anti-maine-law[10] flavor. The littlest children, and I, strolled along the shore while preparations were in progress for our last stage. Two wagons carried off a portion of the party, and the residue entered two sailboats, & the luggage a third. The sail up Somes Sound was rather dull; that is to say some of us napped, and some kept awake; but passages of the route, where we passed between mountains as fine as the Highlands, & tumbling sheer off to the water like Butterhill,[11] were full of interest.

It was near twilight when we came to Somes' & in sight of the flagstaff & flying color. The tide was low, & we therefore made our landing at a point jutting out from a meadow, and walked through a hayfield, and along the road to the house, stringing in Indian file through the cowpath that turned in all directions, making a procession of the gayest sort.

All hands were soon ready to enjoy the supper, and at an early hour every light was out and every voice still.

Here we are at the end of a journey of about 450 miles, safe, and well, except some remnants of seasickness, and stowed most securely and pleasantly in the very middle of this island, the most out of the way piece of land on the northern coast. It was not without sincere thanksgiving, & a hopeful trust, that we laid ourselves down to rest under the shelter of the faithful Father in Heaven.

Thursday. Aug. 2. 1855.

This day was spent in getting things to rights and preparing to stay in our new quarters, and with some strolling among the new scenes. The married people and the young ladies, little girls and nurses are bestowed in Mr. Somes principal house, which also contains the kitchen, dining room & parlors; while the rest of the party lodge in an extra house, & use the whole of it. Our lodgings are rather of the beech nut shape, but airy in this climate, and the housekeeping is as nice as can be. The Someses lodge in a third house. Thus no inconsiderable fraction of the village is subjected to our service.

Our walks brought to light an abundance of wildflowers, and of ornamental plants; the chief of the latter being pigeon or bunch berries, now abundant, in splending[12] clusters which decorate the ladies with singularly pretty effect. My gun — a new one — occupied me much, but I succeeded at last in making it actually go off.

In the afternoon the piano arrived, in a sailboat, and we had a grand time in landing, carting, including unboxing, setting up and trying it. The result was greatly to our delight, the tones being good and the case handsome. The men of the neighborhood turned in as volunteers, to try & lift, and Miss Fay rewarded their civility by playing some common airs on the piano — the first time such an instrument ever sounded in Somesville.

In the evening we gathered in the parlor, and had a charming time with music and books, and conversation.

Friday. August 3. 1855

This morning I took an early look at the east, and saw the coming of the light over the rough mountains. Long before the sun's face was in sight, I could see his rays resting on high grounds west of me; and the hills in the east now looked green, where they are bare rock and almost white in full day.

After breakfast the party mustered in the parlor for devotions, Dr. Stone officiating. He read the Bible and lead us in prayer. His whole manner is excellent, and is a just expression of the fervent piety and deep worship and clear faith that rule in his heart and mind. It is a blessing to have such an one with us, and thus to hold in view the most serious aspect of life, while pursuing needful but engrossing recreation.

All this morning I loitered at the house; and at noon went out with two of the boys to try further experiments with the new gun. Found it was possible to let it off, and tested its accuracy by a mark.

In the afternoon many of the party went off on a tramp. We took the north road, and following along the whole west side of a little lake, not named, and thence through the woods by a delightful shady path, to the end of a long lake, where we sat down and feasted our eyes with the beautiful scene. This lake is about 6 miles long, and from this point we looked its length. It was smooth as a mirror. On each side the banks were an unbroken forest. At the farther end rose up the mountains which line the coast, and from this very point present a most noble outline. The mountains seemed to rise right from the lake. This water has no name. Dr. Stone proposed to call it Lake Silence — significant of its character today. Mr. Church had previously called it Crescent Lake, from the fact that it is of a crescent form.[13]

There are rough sketches of this view, and threats of drawings; but I fear that the memory alone will be changed with the extremely beautiful features of this prospect.

The boys have boated today, and everybody has lounged. The backgammon boards have been opened in the yard, under the trees; and every breath of air has been a luxury.

Saturday. August 4. 1855.

This was a day of varieties. We had clouds, and sun, and showers, and clear weather again. We strolled, and rowed, and read, and fished; and at sundown gathered on a rock back of our quarters to enjoy a sunset of rare beauty and splendor. Mr. Church says this island is remarkable for fine sunsets; and our stay here is daily proving his impression just. There cannot be a description of this sunset; it must be seen.

A short row in the rain was one of the exciting things. Nobody was hurt, and the whole party came home drenched, & deemed themselves fortunate to have such an experience.

The fish would not bite, and so we tried the fishing smack which lay off in the bay, and there the silver hook worked well.

In the evening we had some rehearsals of music for the service of Sunday.

Thus far our stay here has been delightful. The walks are various, & all good. The scene continually before us from our door is one of the finest of landscapes. The children are perfectly overflowing with spirits, and think there never was such a place as Somesville and its vicinity. While our friends at home are sweltering in the heats of August, we find winter clothing not too much in the evening and morning, and the very hottest of the day is not too warm for walking out.[14] The mountain air, the forest air, the sea air, — all combine here, and the compound is deliciously pure. The water too is soft and faultless. We drink it cool from the wells and springs, without need of ice.

The day was opened by our party with the Bible and worship, which is to be the standing appointment during our stay here. Dr. Stone's offices in this respect are most excellent and acceptable.

Sunday. August 5. 1855.

The village church is a fair building with a chalk white steeple. Different denominations joined in erecting it, and in the rotation of ministers it happens that the church will not be open today at all. Dr. Stone has brought no sermons, as he came for rest; and he is not an extemporiser. Consequently he declines to use the church, which was offered to him.

Nevertheless we had a service in our own house, the Doctor officiating in the full morning service of our church, and closing by some remarks on subjects presented by the scriptures read. The piano, and Miss Fay, and all the other Fays, with such help as the party could add, gave us the usual music of our services; and such music as this was, may rarely be heard in any regular church. Miss Fay is leader and director in

Dr. Stone's church, and she both plays and sings with beauty, power and expression, and her brothers each sustain a part and sing beautifully.

Dr. Stone's brief discourse was adapted to our case, and was truly interesting & instructive. Most of the party being Episcopalians, and all having prayer books, the responsive parts of the service were well sustained, and the whole effect — judging from my own sensations, and what I observed of the apparent feeling of others — was truly devotional and religious.

At the close of the afternoon we strolled away on gentle walks, in small parties. A few of us went around the west arms of the harbor, and upon the point where the tide rushes through the "narrows" between the west shore of the "river" and the island opposite our house. On the point I saw a crane standing a few days ago; and as he stood there long, I named it Crane Point.[15] Well, upon Crane Point we stood & waved our handkerchiefs till our friends at the house answered, and sent over the row boat. It was a charming spot, out in the water, with a shelving rock shore, and commanded a lovely prospect on many sides. The boat came, & we glided home over a plain of water as smooth as if frozen in a still night.

In the evening we had evening prayers with psalmody;[16] and before we broke up, the Gloria in Excelsis was sung with great interest, and not without a touch of true emotion.

My reading today has been in Lambruschini; on which I make no comment now.

Monday. August 6. 1855.

This morning Mr. Fay started for Boston. He went to Tremont in a waggon, with Mr. Church, Mary Tracy & Miss Fay; he to take the boat at Tremont, & they to return with the waggon. The first dash of the horse brought him too fast around the turn, and the strap of the seat giving away, Mr. Church went over by a somerset [17] to the ground. Not much hurt, he sprang gaily to his feet, and entered again. Bad luck was with the expedition however, for they reached the end of their journey just five minutes after the boat had gone.

While they were away, I took Fanny & Clara, and Charlie and Clement Fay, off on a tramp to Beech Hill. The gun went along, but such a chattering party prevented any use for it. One poor bird alone came back with us. Beech Hill rises gradually for a mile, and ends in a knoll of rocky ground overlooking a vast field of country. On one side of us lay Lake Silence, or Crescent Lake, — which to the inhabitants there has no name; on the other side sleeps another lake, Dennins Pond — a sheet of water three miles long, shaded with a range of mountains, high, steep, and rocky. On every side beyond, there are farms, bays with vessels sailing in them, villages, coasts of the main land, mountains back from the coast, and all the multiform variety of sound, river, bay, pond, cliff, forest, and farm that belong to the island itself.

As Fanny and Clem lounged under a tree — she to work and he to keep her company & rest himself — while Charlie & Clara & I climbed the last knoll, a kind woman of the neighborhood, came out in bare head & apron, from her work, to offer them berries & milk. She was Mrs. Richardson,[18] and her house was "neat enough for one to eat bread & butter after it had fallen on her floor butter side down." When the rest of us returned, we called on her & added our thanks to theirs, for the very civil and polite treatment they received; and we also made proof of the richness of this milk. The children hardly found words for the expression of their ideas of this milk, which evidently contained no chalk nor water, but much cream, and was in a word, a wonder to New York & Boston boys and girls! Coming home, the waggon quartette overtook us, having returned by a different route; and Mr. Church came out to join the girls & me, & let the boys ride home.

This tramp was accomplished between ten and two o'clock, without shade on the road, in this month of August, in a clear sun; and yet it was comfortable. Such is our air and such our temperature.

In the afternoon we tried our new establishment, the horses and waggon chartered for our use the whole period of our stay. A pair of tough, small, round horses, full of spirit, a long 3 seated waggon, holding 9 persons, rigged with firm springs and a brake, and a driver accustomed to this land of hills and rocks, make up the turnout. We took in Mr. Church, Cordelia Kirkland, and the married people, and drove off towards Newport Mountain. The road is mostly in the woods, and is up and down beyond all my precedents. The brake was all the saving of the establishment, and the way those winged nags flew up the hills was a sight. When we reached Eagle Lake, it was clear that we could not ascend the mountain & return today. So we stopped a long time at the lake. This lake Mr. Church named, from its being so constantly hovered over by eagles. It is a most wild and picturesque spot. We sat at the outlet, where log cutters have flushed the water some three feet, and the sheet lay before us, dark & forest bound, and overhung by several mountains, now near enough to impress us with their vastness. Two huge broad backs of rock, near 2000 feet high [*actually 1,530 ft.*] with five intermediate peaks, some rock, some green with woods, and all crowded between the two chief elevations, make the grand back ground of this lake. Nothing can surpass the beauty and grandeur of the mountain belt, which walls up the sides & head of this quiet undisturbed plain of water. It may well be under the protection of the hills, for it is of their company itself being about 700 feet above the sea & drawing its supplies from the torrents and springs of the overhanging hills themselves. We sat on logs within the margin of the lake, and saw some of the eagles that have suggested its name. The water was cool, and all drank of it.

Soon after we turned away, the sun drew near its western plunge, and a tinge of rosy light came upon the bare side of Newport Mountain, turning its whitened and bone like rocks into a beautiful mass of rosy slopes. It was not a faint, but a strong, tinge of the rosy color, and the mountain looked as gay as if every cliff and craig in it were converted into rose quartz. We soon gained a height from which the sunset itself was visible, and then again we had one of the most superb displays of tinted clouds, and bars of light, over a distant horizon. The whole prospect on our return was wide & commanding; and we were occupied now by the distant mountains on the mainland, and now by the ranges of this island, and now by lakes and ponds, and now by the open vista down the "river" or Somes Sound. This latter view greatly resembles the north end of the Highlands as seen from Newburgh.[19] The hills are of similar form and character; and the greater distance in the present case, makes up for the deficiency of height in the Highlands, and equalizes the effect.

On our way home we roused two hares in the road — it being about the rabbits time of day; and our way out we examined & left a small brown snake, the like of which I never saw before, and also one garter snake. It seems that no venomous serpents exist on the island.

Our evening has gone by blithely. The piano is a standing resource and Mr. Church's capacity for entertainment is perfectly inexhaustible.

I went around as usual to see the boys safe in bed; and then came home to bid our drowsy company good night as they dropped off one by one.

When all others were asleep, I took to my journal, and wrote the hasty entries of Augt. 2nd & thence till now.

A thousand good things come in every day, which ought to go upon the Log Book. They break out at our long table, or in the tramps, or in the parlor, & if we could restore them hereafter they would help us to enjoy again the scenes now passing by.

I must not forget that Charlie is taking lessons in swimming from all the other boys; that Fanny and Clara have been out today in a boat with two of the boys, and have each tried the oars; that not a solitary fish has been caught by any of the party or any of the Somes since we came; and that it is found that all our names can be combined in easy sentences. Thus: — "The table was full when we sat down, but now the Fays from Kirkland, are flitting, and there are left only a few Traceys of a Stone Church." I proposed that we should have a group representing our landing & march up to the house, the doctor in gown, Church in poncho carrying his coffee pot and lamp, Charlie with gun & accoutrements, several of us bearing the piano open, the nurses lugging the little ones, the ladies & boys carrying shawls, bows & arrows, flats, etc., with a small group of young ladies contemplating with wonder the swifts in the fence. Church proposed to paint arms of the party on the waggon, and suggested that it be a group — a pair of Fays, harnessed with Traces, pulling a Stone over a Church. I proposed also the progressive picture of the party, coming here pale conservatives, and going away red republicans: — a state of color to which they are fast approaching.

Tuesday. August 7th. 1855.

A splendid dawn, but I could not induce Fanny to rouse & look at it, although she last night insisted on my waking her. How hard it is to break off ones sleep before the normal hour. The good resolutions of last night, appear as very thin ghosts this morning, and we have little trouble in reconsidering and over ruling them.

This forenoon a small boat load of us went out, fishing, & scenery hunting, & lounging. Mr. Church and I rowed, and the young ladies and little girls made up the residue of the party. We passed beyond the south island, and exercised a vast amount of perseverance, and were rewarded with 3 fishes. We then pulled to the smooth beach, which looked like sand but proved to be wholly of broken stone most beautifully washed and sifted by the breakers. We lounged on shore, gazed down the river and along the mountains, watched the eagles which were near, and finally rowed home.

In the afternoon a waggon load drove over to Seal Cove, stopping at the high ground this side of the cove, where the prospect is perfect. The sun did not shine out, but we had a grand view of mountain and valley, and of lake and sea. Four lakes were in sight at once, including Crescent Lake, the Skating Pond, and a new pond which as James Fay first descried it, we named Loch Fay. This latter pond off to the north of the Seal Cove Road. Returning we gathered pond lillies from the Skating Pond, [20] and wild ferns at its shore, and came home just in time to escape a shower; when we found that the boys had been off all afternoon in the boat, and had had some luck in fishing for eels from the wharf. *

Mr. Fay left us this morning, by the mail stage (waggon) for Ellsworth, whence he goes by land to Boston.

The sun is down, but the haymakers are at work, saving the crop. This island bears very little farm products, save hay, oats & potatoes. There is, here and there, a small corn patch, and once I saw a little buck wheat, and once a small patch of barley — intended, no doubt, for gruel, as they have "made it felony to drink small beer." The people seem to be abundant. The roads are good. The houses are comfortable. There are churches & schoolhouses. This afternoon we found an old mildewed, unpainted church,[21] with a short square tower, and long windows, standing in a large field near a woods. A farmer's harrow was leaning against one side of the church; but they had succeeded in clearing the spot of all trees and shrubs. It was picturesque object, in its form, age and position, and only lacked what it had been industriously deprived of, a few tall spruce trees around it, to render it an object of taste as well as veneration.

The Somes family have been here 90 years. The ancestor came from Gloucester. The master of this house is a man of property & position here. He is now collector of customs for this island, and is much away on his official business. Commerce and fisheries are the business of every body here. A man gets a clearing, a cottage, a yoke of oxen, a cart, and a sloop or schooner. They fish and coast, and build vessels. Consequently the collectorship is a part of duty and service.

This evening it rains and is cool enough to make closed windows agreeable. We met in the parlor after tea and had a grand entertainment with the Dumb Orator, the Sale of Statuary, and proverb guessing. At half past nine I started off the boys and little ones, and at ten the lights were out. We threaten to have a regular time table and to run by it. Breakfast is to be at 7 1/2, dinner at 1, tea at 7 1/2, bed time at 10.

I must note down that the boys have named the little island in the west cove of the bay, Moss Island,[22] from its abundance of mosses.

Our diet here is simple but excellent. Clams & clam chowder are easily had. Fish and fish chowder also. The island produces eggs and milk in great abundance, and these are leading articles of our fare. Then there is occasionally lamb or mutton, and sometimes ham. Coffee made by Mr. Church in his syphon coffeepot, is most exquisite. We also have oolong and congo teas. Blueberries and red raspberries are plenty, with sugar & cream. To this list add hot biscuits, cake of sundry sorts (all good and of the very best quality & style) and clean tumblers of water from the well cold enough without ice.

Wednesday. August 8. 1855.

This day, to my surprise, was announced by the purest silver dawn. We had voted it a wet day, and not fit for an expedition. The sun came off so clear, and the air so fresh, that we determined to make the ascent of Mount Newport, (or Newport Mountain) the highest land on the island. The preparations were extensive. Our party waggon — a sort of omnibus, plurisbusque, — was filled with the supplies in a box on the rack and three boys were seated there. Two other vehicles were obtained, each drawn by one horse, but containing three or four people each. At ten a.m. we drove off — a party of fifteen, with one driver and one boy guide, making 17 in all.

A rough ride to the foot of Eagle Lake was a gay beginning. There we lounged till the driver & guide had taken the horses back to the nearest house, and when the guide returned we set out with basket, pail, shawl, & sunshade, to make the foot passage. First it took us through a broad woods, then up a hillside of green grass with scattered trees, then up the stoney side of the bare mountain. An old forest has once covered the sides of this mountain; but successive fires have bared the surface, except here & there a dead stump, tall & barkless & bleached, and a few patches of woods which the dampness of their lower grounds have saved from the general conflagration, and which at a distance look like cloud shadows. The rock is a grey granite, and its surface is not too steep, where the path lies, to be ascended readily. Many a time did our long train halt, and many a time drag on again, curving prettily along up the mountain path when moving, and seated about on stones and mosses when resting, with a continual groping for whortleberries and the mountain cranberries. The prospect, back of us, grew wider and wider. We soon saw Frenchmans Bay; then the Porcupine Islands; then the eastern quarter of the ocean; and lake after lake upon this island gleamed out of the green below. A treasure of pure cold water was found in a recess of the rock under a huge boulder, from which we drank twice around in the metal cup from my pocket flask. At last we mounted the top, full 2000 feet above the sea, and looked down upon such a prospect as cannot be well described.

To begin, we can trace the water around the entire circumference of this island, a dozen miles broad. Beyond the island, on all sides but one, there are bays, points, promontories, hills, mountains, islands, rocks. It seems as if the whole water front of Maine was in sight, with islands totally innumerable. Some of the islands are bluff rocks, some are wooded darkly, some flat and pale green with pastures. A few white light-houses stand out at the headlands. All over the scene are specks of canvas where the fisherman are gathering or carrying away their harvest. But the ocean side was grandest of all. The vast blue plain swept around a full semi-circle, and came up to the foot of our mountain. The shipping scattered over it, like a few white motes, heightened the tint of blue, & helped us to appreciate the enormous space of ocean under our eyes. By a rough calculation, I find that we could reach within the horizon a semicircle of 110 miles long and 55 miles broad. On the other side, distant mountains peeped above the horizon pale with distance, among which Kitadin [23] was well defined. But spite of all other objects, I must admit myself smitten with that wide, wide, blue ocean, as the most grand, most impressive, most beautiful, and yet most fearful, of all the things in this complete prospect. The very top rock of this pile is surmounted by the observatory of the coast survey, and a surveyor was there, in his thick box coat, taking directions of the endless series of land marks visible from this commanding point. We stopped at his shanty, where he passes the storms and the nights, and there opened our stores for our midday repast. The treasures in the basket & pail, when spread out, seemed to be ten times as much, and the quality was most attractive. Nothing was left over.

This mountain has its steep sides as well as slopes, and one of the precipices seemed to drop down full a thousand feet with a wild, chilly, hopeless looking valley, which was guarded by a steep wall on the opposite side. It was fearful chasm to look down into, and the loosened fragments of rock at its summit seemed ready to start for a plunge into the glen below. It was peculiar that Clement & Charlie, the two youngest of the party, were totally attracted by this precipice & chasm, and insisted on all coming to look down, from behind a parapet they had discovered at the brink.

The air here was delicious. No smell of streets, or gasworks, nor of mud left bare by low tide, nor of fields, nor of forests, nor of smoke. The breeze came clear out of the sky, far above everything but the clouds, and was chemically perfect. In this August day we wore woolens here, and took shelter from the wind, in the clear sunshine.

Small bushes, ferns, grass & cranberries abound on this summit, and the whortleberries[24] were the largest in size, and the best in flavor, and the most numerous in the cluster, of any we have ever seen.

But I come around again to the ocean. There it is, wide, blue, level, — a whole world out spread — the counterpart of the vast blue sky above. It looks tranquil, but proof of its rolling is seen on some reefs, where the long white line of breakers fades & brightens as we watch it. Some vessels not far from land leave a faint track on the plain. One steamer, the *Rockland*, looks like a sea bug, and on watching it, like a clock finger, we can see it actually moves. But the broad plain is little spotted with these tiny works of man, and its great solemn face turns up with a sublime and heavenward gaze. Old as the world, and yet as fresh and living as if newly finished. The little excitements and contests and hopes and doubts of the human world, sink into nothing as we look out upon the mighty world of waters. Time, and showers, and frost, have scarred these old rocks, and turned the very granite into mud and sand; but the sea is unchanged. Heat, cold, storm, calm, sun, rain, in thousands of years, have wrought no alteration in its quality or looks; but the first eyes which looked out from this peak saw the ocean as we see it now; and the last that shall gaze here, wondering like us, will find it as it is today.

Down from the mountain, and from the contemplative, away we go. Hold on! — a book is lost! What book? What should it be but a volume of Don Quixote, which a La Mancha like girl has brought up here in her pocket. She was even reading this book, with the sea right before her face! Some blueberries drew her from the superior charms of Quixotism, and while plunging for the fruits she parted with the knight. We rambled in hunting for the book, as for a pin in a stubblefield, but left it to be gnawed by rabbits, dissolved by showers, and finally to mingle itself in the substance of moss and lichens.

Away again. What fun to go down on the same path where we tugged up. Few halts, few chances for story tellers, but many a happy saying, and we were shortly across the gray and the green, and winding through the woods.

The waggons somehow would not hold their former load. There was a grand fuss, and finally two boys got a passage in a fourth waggon with a racing fellow who chanced along and welcomed them. To end all, soon after we started up, Mr. Church leapt out and ran ahead of us; and when we reached home he had beaten us on the five mile heat, by walking and running, and seemed as fresh as morning.

The news was upon us in a minute. Mr. Winthrop had arrived to join the party; and the three boys who had staid home had caught 28 fishes in the bay. Conversation opened richly, and we all met at tea table, and then in the parlor feeling that the day had been one of greatest interest and pleasure.

It is funny to watch the changing color, and even the coating, of the party. Fiery streaks, pealed skins, freckles, & brown hands, are coming along very fast.

By 10 o'clock the lights were out.

Thursday. August 9. 1855.

It rains. It blows. From my window I can see eight fishing vessels which have come up into our bay to escape the storm. The water is full of white caps.

All hands are driven in; and so with our party. The boys are playing gymics,[25] the children playing tea — real as to all but the herb-drink, the young ladies are sewing, the gentlemen are tinkering, and writing up the log book, or reading aloud to the lady sewers. We brought some books, but the family library of the house is very good & ample. Our piano holds out good, and we have players of exquisite taste and great skill. An open fire of wood in our second parlor casts a cheerful light, and a welcome warmth. So howl on storm! The vessels are safely moored, the house is tight and warm, and the dinner to come sends up a savory smell. Nod away bushes and mountain ash, shake your arms and curve your fingers old willows, patter & drip you rain drops, "wheugh" back to you Wind; I am content to bide your time, and you may have your romping out to your heart's content.

All the forenoon I was between this diary and the parlor, and only saw and heard a part of the entertainment of the company, in reading, music, dancing, and games. Mr. Winthrop has become a favorite immediately, and he enters into every thing with true zest.

At dinner table Mr. Church announced his design of going today to Schooner Head, to see the beating of the storm on the rocky shore. I wished much to join him, but concluded that it was not fair to go away for this rainy day and all of tomorrow, and leave Mr. Winthrop to entertain & be entertained in a company all new to him. In the end, James Fay & Church made the start in the single waggon well shielded from the rain.

While the party were lounging after dinner I executed my threat of putting Fanny in verse, and hurried down with my manuscript in pocket as rough as drafted, without even dividing the lines. We had a frolicksome dance as much to the entertainment of the beholders as the exercise of the performers. After this was over, I called up Fanny and read my verses to the company.

Here they are:

To Newport Mountain a party went,
A party fifteen strong;
On prospect-viewing all were bent;
And Fanny was along.
Now over the roads
Rattled the loads,
In waggons three;
Now out they dump,
And stump over stump

To the greenwood tree.

~

Up through the forest they tramp,
Over the grassy walk,
Through the rooty swamp,
Up the steep roof of rock;
Till by the cloud
Shouts a hurra loud,
The Sea, the Sea!
Then wild they rush
Till past the last bush,
And old Ocean they see.

~

Out on the craig the party sat,
A party fifteen strong,
Prospect viewing they were at;
And Fanny was along.
The sky was blue,
And the ocean too,
Facing south-east;
And there she read,
Holding her head,
Fronting south-east.

~

Cervantes, Ocean yields to you,
Old Ocean blue and wide,
Don Quixote is more true
To the dreamers than the tide.
The book is read;

With giddy head,
She jumps away;
Book's on the ground,
Tis never found,
Alack-a-day!

This took so pleasantly that I was forced to read it a second time. Then behold! Mr. Winthrop was emboldened to draw from his pocket some verses he had composed on the subject of the lost book, and which were roughly put on brown paper. Being twice read to our great gratification, I have the paper to copy in this log book, here are the verses of Mr. Winthrop:

~

Who lost the book?
"Not I" with a look
Of Calmness said Mrs. Stone;
"I went for a walk
"And a view and a talk
"To a grand old mountain lone."

~

Who lost the book?
"Why, who ever took
"A romance where nature was racy,
"When each day we are able
"To read at a table
"Or desk," said Mr. Tracy.

~

Who lost the book?
"To a lovely nook
"Of an island we've stolen away;
"We're taught by the breeze

"And the grand broad seas
"Not by printed words," said Miss Fay.

~

Who lost the book?
"Twas a tale of a joke
"Played in Spain that wild mirkland,
"Of a sort of sham knight,
"Don Quixote hight.[26]
"I don't like dull jokes," said Miss Kirkland.

~

Who lost the book?
Why, Kent, you took
Something slyly out of your pocket;
And as we can't find
Anything of the kind,
Have you pushed it off of the docket?

~

Who lost the book?
For we cannot brook
To be kept thus in the lurch.
If you are dull
Our pleasure is null;
We shall have to read, Mr. Church.

~

Who lost the book?
There not even a rock
Or a raven, a bird that is canny,
Can find it, it lies
Near the welkin of skies.
"I lost it," said boldly Miss Fanny.

The rest of the afternoon went off quietly, between reading and sewing, and the juvenile plays of the boys. Before tea time the wind ceased, and the fog came over the bay, promising a favorable change for tomorrow.

The evening has been enlivened with music, and charades and proverbs and characters. One of the charades was Don Quixote (-Don. quick, sot.-) and another "Log Book"; both which, as well as the others, went off charmingly.

At an early hour we retire: - the young ladies having the promise of my hands as rower if they give me fifteen minutes notice, at any hour of the early tide tomorrow morning.

Friday. August 10. 1855

The rain and fog have passed. The east was glaring at 4 o'clock, and by half past six the sun was pouring down. Cordelia went out to walk about that time, "solitary and alone." The harbor is like a mirror. The smacks[27] will soon weigh anchor and sail away.

In the morning Mr. Winthrop & I took all the ladies who would go, in two waggons, to Seal Cove. The single horse was wanted by his owner at a certain hour, and I therefore changed with Mr. Winthrop and brought back Louisa and Julia in the little waggon, while he went to finish the trip by driving down to the Cove, & home by Beech Hill. The air and light were very fine and inspiring, and the ladies sang all the way, in an endless succession of glees and ditties. The sea, or rather the small bays, which came in sight, were rolling finely before a North West wind, and the caps were plenty & sparkling.

Returning, we met Mr. Church & James Fay who had gone around to Schooner head,[28] seen the rolling of the ocean, and the wild precipices there, and also two wild deer. The great wonder — Nancy Jane was not at home, but the other — Charles William — was seen and admired. The same old clock was found going, and the same family were there in the curious but nice house in the quiet out of the way nook. Mr. Church brought home 50 mackerel — size no. 3, — a welcome help to our bill of fare.

The boys have been out in the boat, and came in about the same time, with a fine show of flounders & other fish.

In the afternoon Mr. Church and I, with Mrs. Stone, took the youngest boys, & Fanny & Clara, around the bay by waggon. This was our first drive down the northeast harbor road — or the road on the east side of Somes Sound. A novel and imposing scene opened on us as we reached the mountain belt that stretches along back of the seashore. We entered between two mountains, by a notch so wild and bold, that I was reminded of Franconia at every step. A long, steep overhanging ridge of rock on our right, partly hidden (& thereby magnified) by scattering trees, with here and there a great bare sloping roof of granite, striped but not grooved with the trickling moisture, and with not a few of the rough blocks which had parted from the beetling top, and caught a footing in the side of the mountain. On the left, there was first a mountain, then a craig, then a wood, & then a lake.[29] The lake was a beauty. It lay under the great right hand mountain already mentioned, and was girt about on the other sides by a belt of rocky piles of most unique & picturesque character, being a series of high hills of rock in close order, or perhaps more properly one grand mountain bent around the lake and indented partially from the top line. It is a lake not much short of a mile long, and of fair width, yet yielding a mere rill to its outlet stream. We went to the foot of it, and took a full view of the surroundings, while the sun, near its setting, cast glare and shadow over the bold heads and sides of the mountains, and developed to the eye every feature of their conformation. The time did not suffice for us to drive a mile or two further, and look out on the Ocean. We drove home in a clear cool evening air, witnessing a brilliant but cold sunset, full of pale yellow and lemon color, but destitute of red warmth. The spirits of the children were grand, going & coming; and we all came home feeling as if there was no end to the treasures of this island. The lake I named Notch: — Lake Notch — from its position.

Today a gigantic gentleman appeared from the stage and quartered himself on the village. I now learn that he comes here to fish in Eagle Lake, and will go to live at the house near there for the convenience of the house, & the boats which are owned there. The news comes also, that 25 trout were caught in that lake yesterday.

The first Times came today, dated on the 7th inst. & the 8th with it. No other Times. I had Evening Posts of the 2nd & 8th, & a few intermediate dates today; but no letters. The circle who witnessed the opening of the mail was small, but showed the true New England type of people and of names.

This evening it was cool enough for a fire. We had our full parlor entertained with music, and roasting, and changing seats, and hobknob, & charades; and perpetual interludes of anecdotes and repartees. The evening is short, for we start a division at 9:30 & clear the room at 10. The night till about 10 was very clear. The Milky Way stared down as plainly as a star, and the constellations were readable. It is one of the meteor nights — St. Lawrence day — and we have casually seen a great many shooting stars during the evening. By ten o'clock, a cloud and shower closed our chances for further displays in the heavens.

If it is clear tomorrow, we shall try to make the ascent of the mountains[30] east of — Lake Notch, at least far enough to see the lake of the mountains which lies very far up the steeps. There is no guide nor path; but from what we have seen today, there will be no difficulty in Mr. Church or me leading the party up safely. I regret now that I did not bring a thermometer graduated up to the boiling point; by means of which we could determine the altitude of the high lake.

11:45 pm All clear again. Jupiter and all the stars are bright. No meteors.

Saturday. August 11. 1855.

A cool morning. Wind without rain, but clouds everywhere.

The swing, and short walks, and the hay waggon, and the newspapers, and an early dinner bring us to 2 o'clock. Shuttle cocks, graces, and the like, are a good resource, and much resorted to by the young ladies.

This afternoon there is some sun light, and we may strike off on a good trip some whither.

The drive was to the bridge on the road to Ellsworth. Two waggons drove over to the main land, and came back gratified with a fine country like view.

L. & I walked out a few miles on the same road, until we saw the northern waters, & the main beyond, and many mountains in the wide horizon. Mr. Winthrop joined us, and we had a good time. There are no fruit trees but apple, and very few and scragged are the apple trees. The island must be subject to severe winds in winter, but it cannot have a low range of thermometer in this unfreezing Atlantic. As we approach the mainland, the farms widen & improve, and the buildings multiply.

The evening is unfortunate for the shooting stars. There are many clouds flying, and not enough clear sky to show the meteors, if they come.

Annie is so well and strong today that I feel courageous. The island has done wonders for all the rest, and it seemed strange that she should not be well.

This evening's entertainments have been charades—"Courtship"—and "Indolence." The scenes were carried out with comic improvised dialogues & action, and furnished great amusement. This sort of gaiety, limited as it is, to a short time, & given and received without infringement of one good rule of right living and right feeling, is vastly better for our purposes here than quiet reading. It is also a good lesson to the young, on the facility of entertainment, fully gratifying the mirthful sense, without a teaching upon the rules of virtue and strict propriety.

I went as usual with Charlie & the little boys to the clubhouse (as they call it) and saw them safe in bed. About 10 o'clock, the company retired, & now at 11, the house is still. It is rumored that the young ladies were up & chatting till 2 a.m. last night: if so, they will soon be asleep now.

Sunday. August 12. 1855.

The drowsy influence prevailed this morning. We breakfasted a little before 9 o'clock. It was a charming fresh forenoon. At half past ten all went to Church — the village church, — and were seated in 5 slips taken for the purpose by Mr. Somes. The interior of the church is plain, but very neat, and the congregation were a well dressed but hardy looking people. The minister interested us all. He had nothing provincial in his voice or tone or language, and did not look like the inhabitants of this region. I thought he must be within one generation from the Germans, and his name, Bowker, aids this surmise.These externals favored the ministerial arts, the reading of the bible, the offering of prayers and the delivery of sermons, in which all were gratified and pleased. The ancient puritan usage of standing in prayer and sitting in singing is not lost here, the only modification of it being the rising of the people in the last hymn in the afternoon, and very irreverently turning round so as to face the choir.

The usual intermission of half an hour was today doubled; and we took a light luncheon before the second service. After the second service, at three o'clock we were summoned to an excellent dinner; the luxuries including a delicious lobster salad, and a tapioca custard, and the fresh mountain cranberries.

Dinner being over, the mountains across the bay presented the rare and beautiful spectacle of the clouds passing between & beneath the tops of the mountains, and casting their moving shadows on the broad hill sides. This lasted till sunset, and was continually attracting attention by new phases. Many of us walked across to the hill below Crane Point where the Hay Stack Rocks stand out, and sat there some time...

This evening, after a late tea, we spent the evening together in the parlor, and had charming singing from the ladies & the boys.

I have been pushing along in Lambruschini, and am penetrated with wonder at the zeal with which the absurd dogma is maintained by the shallowest show of reasoning, and the most impious distortions of scripture, as well as by the cheap jugglery of modern romish miracles. The present state of the Roman church is a psychological puzzle: a mystery of abominations, - a wonderful & curious combination of things in flagrant hostility to the divine will and appointments.[31]

Monday. Augt. 13. 1855.

Cloudy & showery this morning. We had reading, music, swinging, hayrack riding, basket making, walking and short rowing; and the boys fished.

This afternoon hot and clear. A load went to the Notch, & saw the lake. I made all go who would, & had not been there before; and the returned party agreed in our praise of the rare scenery there. I strolled away alone, and groped for game with poor success.

This evening we had music, without more gay pastime. We are saddened by the necessity of losing Dr. Stone tomorrow morning. The younger children left at home, threatened with whooping cough, have given the Dr. & Mrs. Stone considerable anxiety at times, and by letters received today they find the state of the posterity such that the parents feel bound to go home immediately. The Doctor's conversation, & whole life before us, mark him as a true and efficient man in his vocation. Mrs. Stone's quiet and gentle manner has given grace to our circle. The boys are good fellows. The two youngest go home, but the eldest, Kent, will stay. They go early tomorrow, in the party's waggon, to Ellsworth, & thence by stage.

The clouds today, several times, have been below the mountains. Our boys had grand luck in fishing, and a stranger showed us this evening a trout of 2 to 3 pounds weight caught today in Eagle Lake.

This evening Mr. Church let off some very pretty fireworks, as a winding up of the boys visit.

Annie seems entirely well and strong; and all the family are growing red and brown. My own strength gains daily, and I little mind the tramping and rowing which would have been hard for me before the vacation began.

I must not omit an entry of the striking resemblance between Dr. Stone and my good uncle George Huntington.[32] They look alike, think like, talk alike, laugh alike. Dr. Stone is a shade the less, in all those respects, but greatly alike. He has the warmth and kindness, but not so much sprightliness & keenness, nor so much of contagious mental & social activity. I had a long conversation with him today, about catholic superstition, mariolatry,[33] & the like, in all which his good sense and true spirituality came out clearly.

I have dispatched Lambruschini: am glad I read it: for now I see the inner mind of that complex body which calls itself the church, yet is the synagogue of Satan.

Tuesday. Augt. 14. 1855.

Mr. Winthrop & I left the party today, and took our way on foot to the great mountain opposite the village, which I now learn is known as Sargent Mountain. We walked briskly to its base, and commenced the ascent. For a mile or more we encountered a close thicket, not broken by a cow path, but only alternated with regions of boulders, stumps, and rotting brush. It was a very hard scramble until we reached the region where the mainland opened upon our view. Then it was steep, rough, & trackless. Once as we sat gazing back on the widened prospect, an eagle soared up near us and perched on a dead tree about two gunshots distant and after exchanging looks with us wheeled off around the mountain. The question whether a lady could make the ascent was fully decided in the negative, with an exception in favor of leather bloomers. We sought for the best patch or route, but found all alike forbidding. The mountain is cut and grooved by ravines, which cannot be avoided without long detours. We clambered up one head which promised a view of the Summit Lake,[34] but did not reveal it. Then we descended into a gorge, & went up the highest point. Here we had almost the view from Newport Mountain; but the defect of the northeast quarter, cut off by the superior height of Newport, is quite a draw back. At the very top rock some one has sat up a boulder and pile of stones. We were ready now for our repast, and finding a small basin at the summit, containing a few gallons of pure, cold water, we filled our cup and seated ourselves on the ocean side of a rock by a bed of whortleberries, and proceeded to our biscuits & raisins.

The air was perfectly clear; and the vast blue ocean spreading out its immense plain, spangled here and there with specks of white sails, and lying in sublime repose, was a theme for solitude and those silent thoughts which draw the soul out from the little circle of human cares to the grand and everlasting harmony of nature. It was easy, and tempting, to count those silvery motes of sails, till my naked eye numbered 55, and I concluded that a telescope would have carried that number four times as high;[35] and it was exciting to descry the far off Mt. Desert Rock[36] — 25 miles from shore — now looking like a pale short line near the horizon; but the great impression of the eternal sea which surrounds and holds the world, came rolling back with its overpowering spring-tide to whelm all ordinary emotions.

This mountain top furnished blueberries of remarkable size, abundance & quality, red raspberries of the best quality, mountain cranberries, pigeon berries, and some bitter cherries; giving out a large choice for our dessert.

Judging by the eye, with aid of the Sea horizon, Newport Mountain is about 300 feet higher than this. It has also a more regular form and gives the eye a full horizon of sea or distant hills.

We were in no hurry, and therefore took a different route down the mountain, seeking for a path fit for ladies to follow. A long way down the northeastern spur, we found the rocks bare and sloping, just as we wanted them; but below that, among the dead posts, and crackling bush, and thick set bushes, the best route was savage. I came out to the clearing with my drilling pantaloons gaping at both knees, and had to resort to pins to make me fit for the highway.

Reaching home at supper time, we found Mr. Church had entertained the party hugely by a series of caricature delineations of our operations, taking us as - two hunters. The whole 17 numbers[37] are funny and witty, and artistic, and amused us as well as all others. [See pages 81 to109 which follow]

The evening entertainments of the parlor were animated; and all dispersed by ten o'clock ready for the long sleep which these scenes produce.

The *Log Book* continues on page 113.

The Tale of Two Hunters

by F. E. Church

Nineteen witty sketches of "two hunters," Charles Tracy ("Mr. T.") and Theodore Winthrop ("Mr. W.") — a continuous narrative.

See reference on the preceding page.

T and W as they appeared starting on a hunting expedition
A neighbor's dog volunteers.

They make a regular stampede in a swamp in a vain search for birds. The dog being disgusted trots homeward.

Both discover game at the same instant and miss.

Charging each other with awkwardness and with disturbing the game prematurely, they exercise themselves into a slight altercation.

Falling into a deep morass, they exhibit astonishing pluck.

The reconciliation.

Leaving the low ground they resort to the high. Not meeting with much Success, they conclude to separate in order to cover more ground.

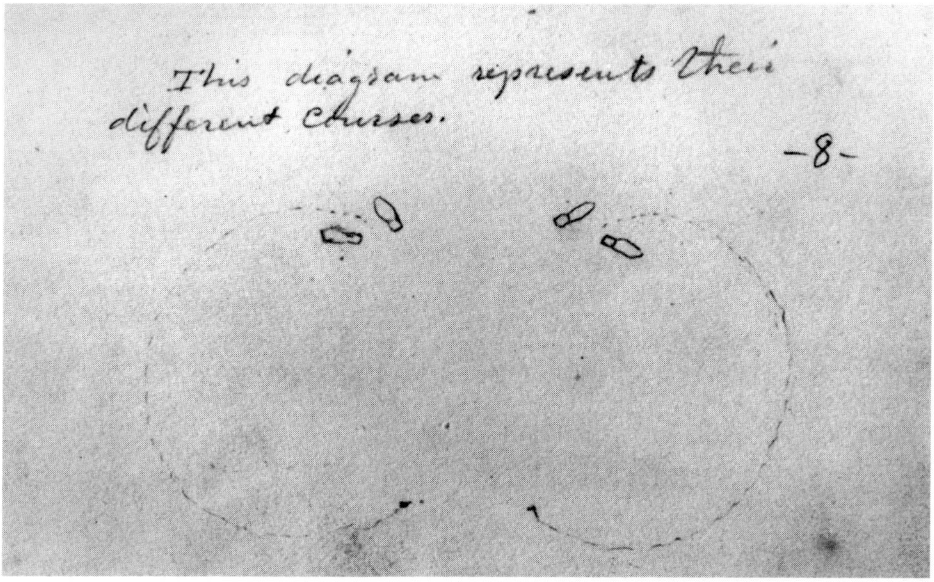

This diagram represents their different courses.

Simultaneously they each discover a Buck.

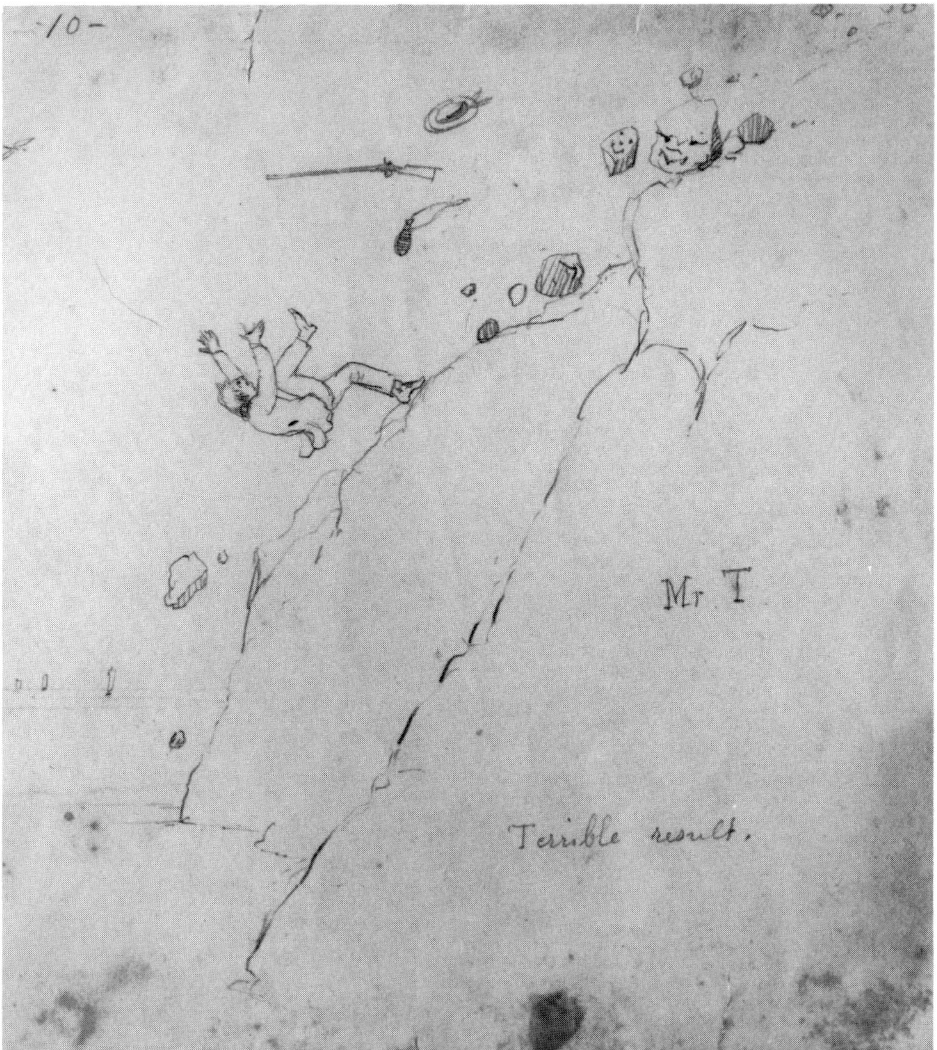

Mr. T. — Terrible result.

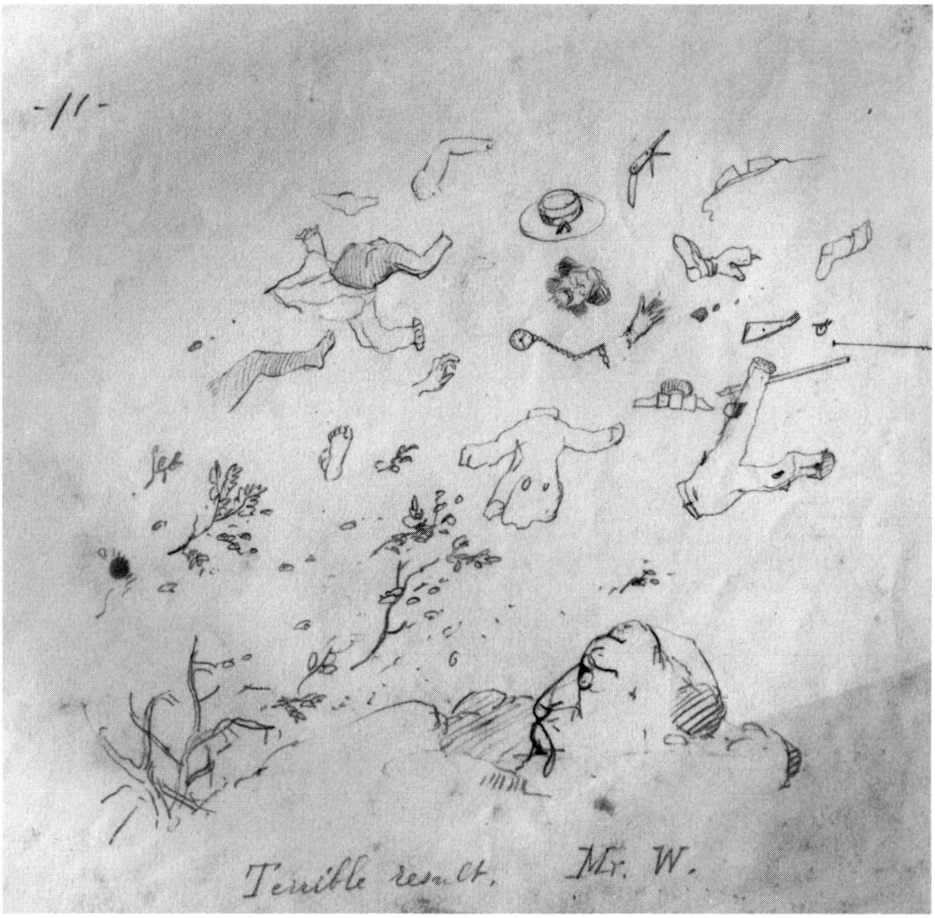

Terrible result. Mr. W.

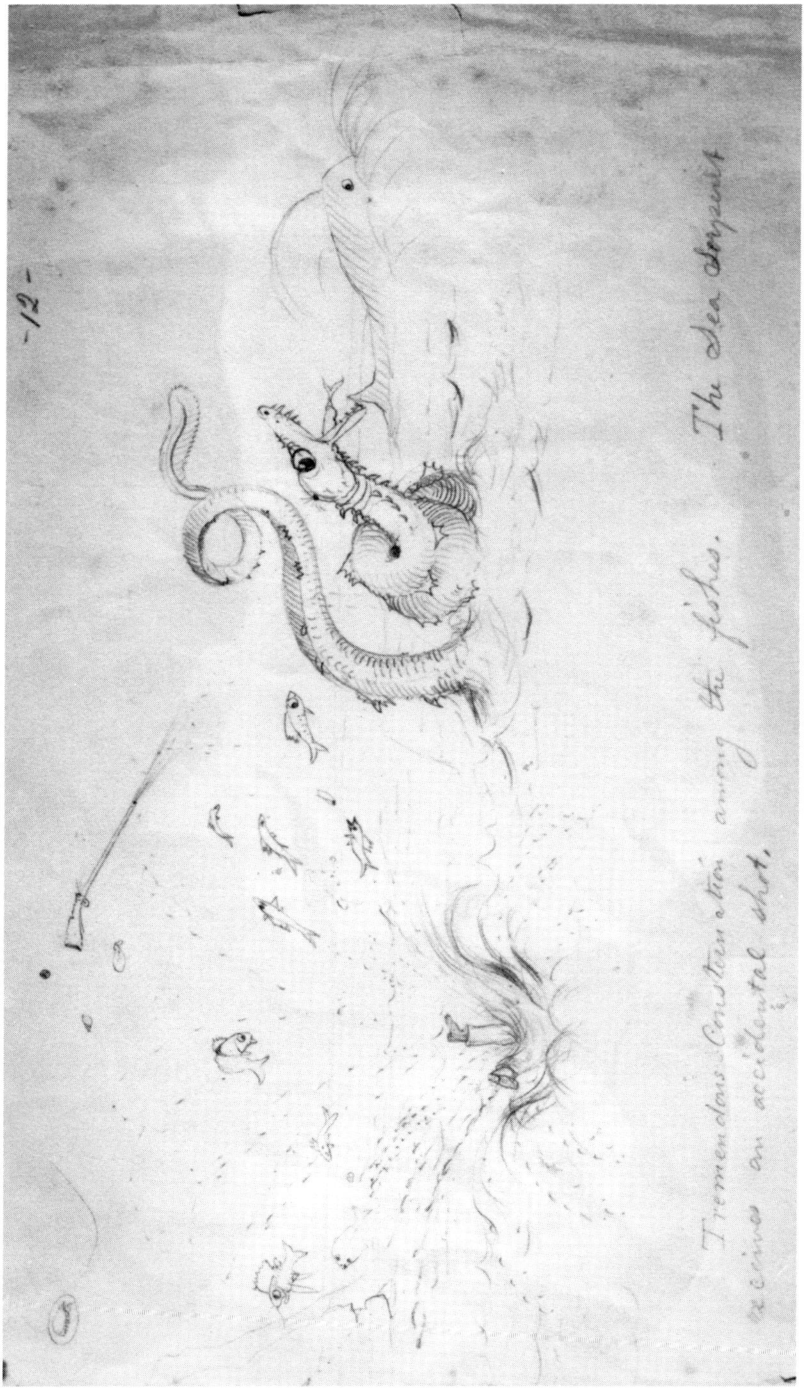

Tremendous consternation among the fishes. The Sea Serpent receives an accidental shot.

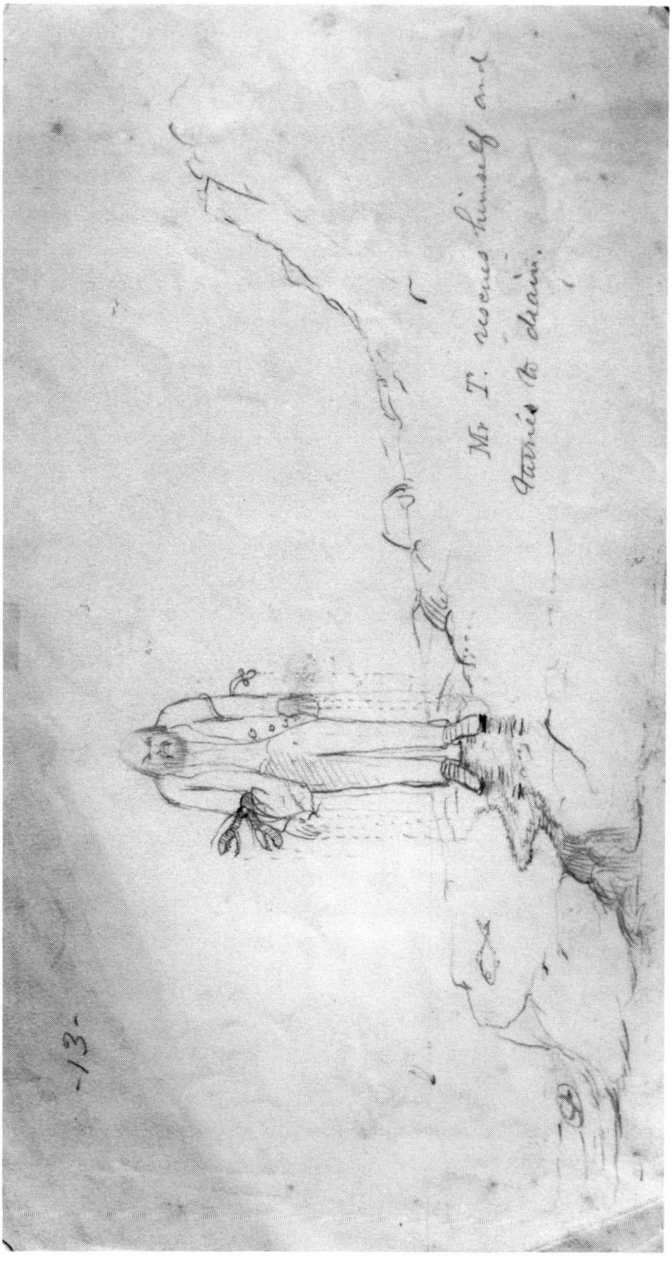

Mr. T. rescues himself and tarries to drain.

Mr. T. makes a search for Mr. W.

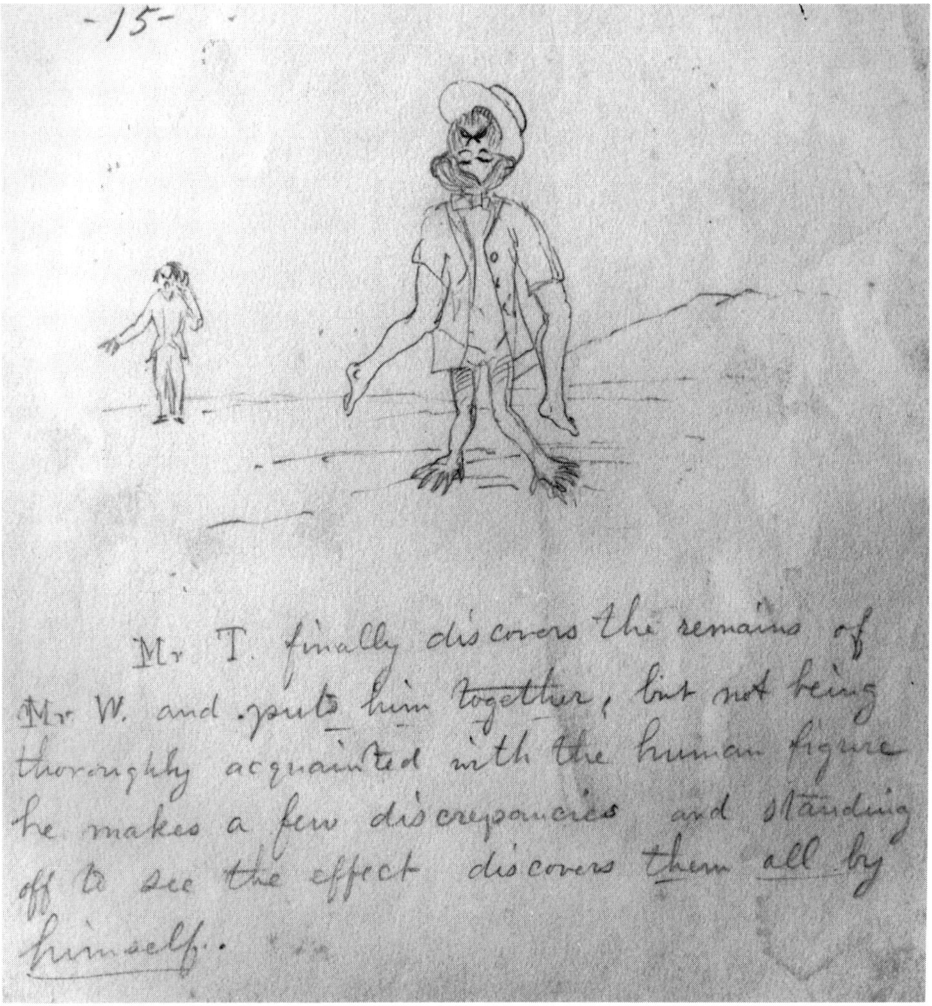

Mr. T finally discovers the remains of Mr. W and puts him together, but not being thoroughly acquainted with the human figure he makes a few discrepancies and standing off to see the effect discovers them all by himself.

The preceding difficulty being overcome they discover the dead sea serpent on the Beach.

Amazed at his vast length they resolve to measure by paces.

They still continue their measurement.

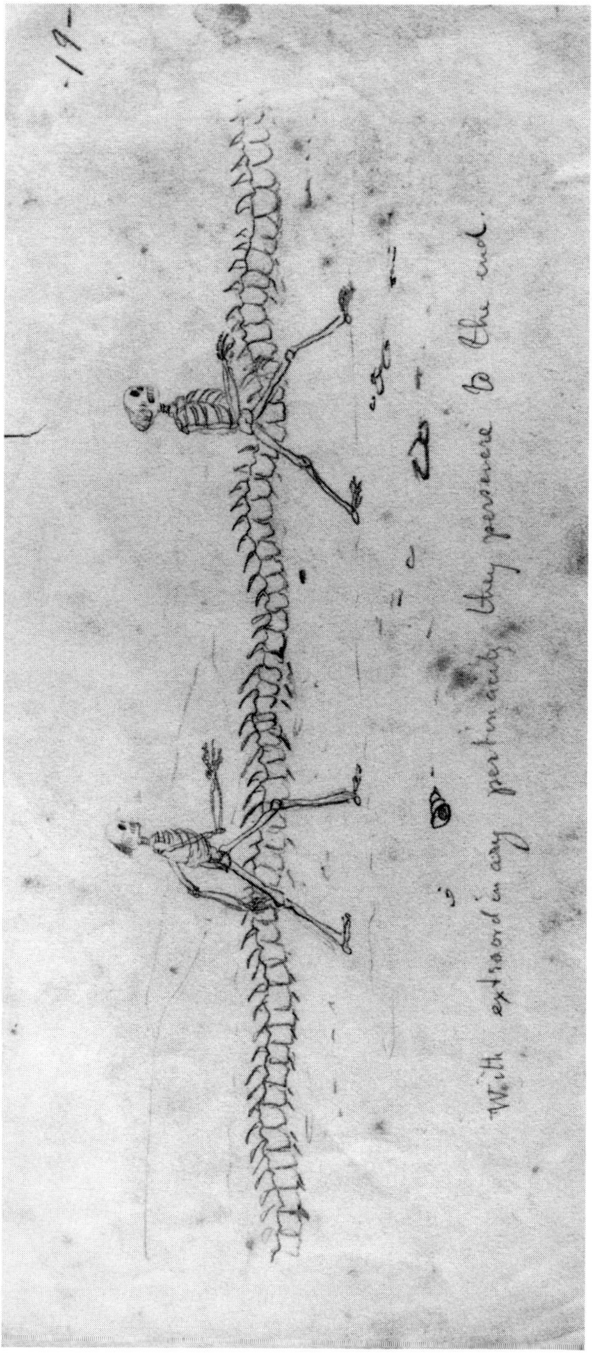

With extraordinary pertinacity they persevere to the end.

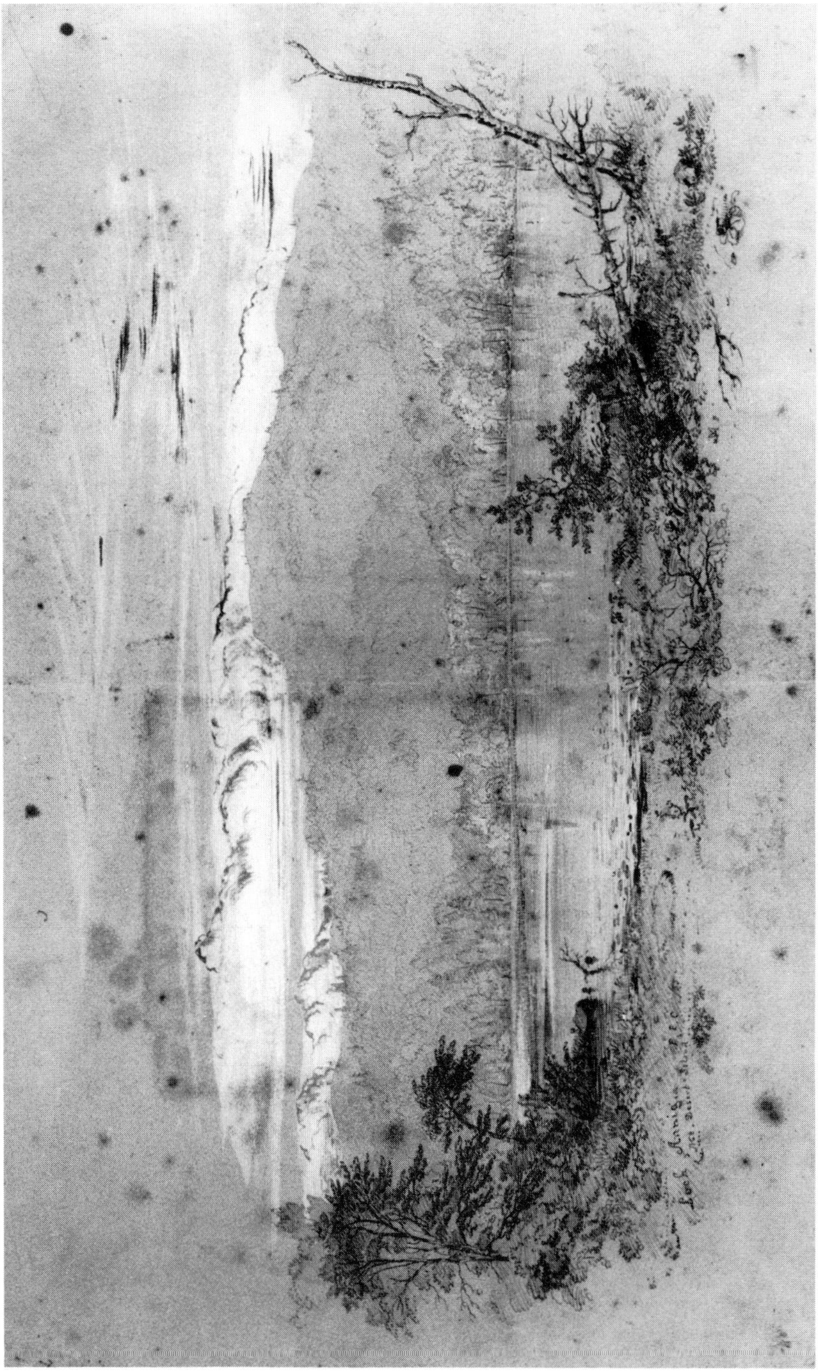

Inscribed ~ Loch Annie   F. E. C. / 55   Mt. Desert Island

Wednesday. August 15. 1855.

This day completes our full fortnight here, and should be marked with a white stone. It has moreover the best title to distinction; for we have made the trip to Bar Harbor, and to Schooner Head & Mr. Lynam's. A drive of 8 miles brought us to Roberts' at Bar Harbor; and there we fished, and strolled, and dined. A most lovely spot it is, — the ocean, the bay, the islands, the rocky shore; — but the place of all was Schooner Head. One of the span[38] needed a shoe, and so we left the great waggon, & putting some least able to walk into the little waggons, we set out, the rest of us on foot. A mile of common road brought us into the woods, and there the road was an ancient one, but so little used that it was clean turf like a pasture. The beauty of such a road, level & green, & trackless, winding through a high wood which stood sheer up at each side, can hardly be imagined without seeing it. As we pressed on, there gradually arose on our right an enormous precipice, a steep mountain side[39] of 1200 ft. seen here and there through the trees, and at last almost overhanging us. There were spots in the wood, where an acre or more of land opened on us from the left, carpeted with grass and barely ornamented with a few trees. Drawing near Schooner Head, the woods grew more open, the trees more broad and spreading, and the grass closer. Here was an Acadian scene of the richest character. The open woods, the open grass fields, the meadow beyond, the ocean in the distance, and on the other side the great dark precipice, were enchanting. The party straggling in, in waggons and on foot, and coming to the last opening were in ecstasy.

Just here I met a girl of about 15, — who said she was a granddaughter of Mr. Lynam, — and on introducing Miss Church and myself, (who were the first arrived), we went together to the house. This girl has the Italian look, and is quite pretty; — especially as animation for Acadian scenery.

Our party assembled at the house, and saw this family in their extremely neat abode. While the bread and milk was preparing, we took the circuit of the rocky head itself. Crossing the meadow, we met Mr. Lynam, the patriarch, whose life began here, and whose sixty years have passed on this spot; and we all were struck with his strong and superior countenance and bearing. On being introduced to him, as Mr. Tracy, he repeated the name, and said his first wife was a Tracy. Not feeling quite at leisure for genealogies, I left it for another day to trace out the descent of Nancy Jane and Charles William, the prodigies of size which inherit the blood of the Traceys.

Leaving the meadow, we ran up the hill to the precipice which over looks the ocean. This point stands out into the sea, and is faced with a craig front of about 75 feet in height, battered and furrowed by the eternal dash of the waves, and jagged into all kinds of notches, and crypts and towers. Strolling over this wild brink we passed around the projecting head, and reached a frightful chasm. The rock front seems to have split off and moved a few feet into the sea, leaving a ghastly fissure; and the outer wall thus formed, has a natural doorway opening through from the sea to the fissure. We crept down the natural steps outside of this guard wall, and passed through the arched doorway to the bottom of the fissure, where every wave rushes up and retreats by the side of our very steps. It is difficult to describe so strangely shaped a thing; but I thought the door way itself constituted a cavern fully 12 feet wide, 15 feet long, and arched from 3 to 10 feet high. Returning to the day above, with shells gathered in the crypt, we were tempted to linger on the rocks and gaze at the wide sweeping sea, which broke quite at our feet; but the necessary haste to return brought us off.[40]

Reaching the house we found our great waggon arrived. The table was set in the "square room," covered with a snow white cloth, and furnished with the most superb of milk and brown wheat bread, & rye & Indian bread, & whortleberries. All feasted and praised the fare. We even penetrated the pantry, and milk room and admired the intense neatness of everything. The milk pitchers continued to go out empty & come back full, until all hands were provisioned for our toilsome return. The young ladies wished to stay over the night, but the house was too full, and all had to come away with us.

Among other prodigies of the locality we saw a baby boy trotting about the grounds on his feet, and learned that he was now 10 months old, and had been so on foot for a whole month.

Mr. Church wished to reach Bar Harbor before us, and therefore hurried on afoot; by means of which he came upon a wild deer and saw him escape.

Crossing the woods, about dark, we started a rabbit; and I had time to cap my gun and shoot him. He crept slowly off into the thicket before we could get to him, and it was too dark to find him.

Several of us walked from three to six miles on this return, and half the party walked four miles on going out. At last, at 9 p.m. we all landed at Somesville safe and sound, hungry and tired; and soon after supper the "Club House" and "Belle Harbor" were as quiet as the stars above them.

I must not omit the meteors, of which we saw several this evening, all ranging from the radiant Mr. Herrick determined for the shooting stars of Augt. 10th.

We had at once a silver new moon, a bright evening star in the west, Jupiter most grand in the east reflected on the bay, the Milky Way well defined and luminous, and an aurora borealis.

Clement Fay, and the little girls, Fanny Fay and Julia Tracy, with their nurses, had kept the day at the house and reported it as very pleasant.

Thursday. Augt. 16. 1855.

A late arrival from "Belle Harbor" completed our company at the breakfast table. Everybody seems inclined to quiet occupations this morning. The ladies sew, the children play backgammon, the gentlemen read and chat.

The very prospect is taking a rest; the top of the mountains has been in the clouds all morning. The boys are off in a boat, on a clam bake.

This afternoon all the youngest girls, with the mammas & me, drove out to the mainland bridge, seeing the cranes, the eagles, and one rabbit. The fog did not hinder our view of objects near at hand; and I therefore preferred the route which afforded the most of near objects of interest.

Meantime the young ladies & gentlemen went into the bay and caught a great quantity of fishes, including some twenty or more mackerel.

This evening the parlor has been cheerful with music, dances, and games.

Annie has felt poorly all day. Tonight she has a fever, and I hope the attack will prove to be a mere cold & will go away with the night. It grieves me to think that she has not been entirely well since we arrived on the island, although she left home unusually well & strong. I think she has grown considerably since the first of July, and I am half impressed with the idea that the present illness is an effect of such rapid growth. Yesterday she weighed 135 lbs. which is more than her mother ever did, & more by 9 lbs. than Mary does now. The foggy atmosphere of today has doubtless put her back.

After all, such an illness, in her case, troubles me; and I look with anxiety for the result.

Friday. Augt. 17. 1855.

Annie slept well, and feels better, but must be still today.

It is a foggy, lowery morning, and the ladies will stay in the house. I fulfill my promise to Charlie & go out "mackereling" with the boys.

Four of us caught 53 mackerel. It rained and blew & rolled, but the boys persevered; and we came home at 2 p.m. in a clear atmosphere.

This afternoon Mr. Church & Mr. Winthrop are out in the boat with the ladies, fishing; and the surplus above a boat load are driving out in the waggon.

Annie is quiet on the bed in our room, and Mrs. Fay is below, and the littles & nurses without, while Louisa and I go off for a walk.

The mail has brought me 6 papers today, — all which seemed unusually flat and abolitionish, — and a letter from Mr. Olmstead which reports affairs at the office in a favorable state.

The fog today is a pretty study. Now it creeps up the hill tops and floats away as clouds, now it steams along over the water of the bay, and now it hides base and summit of the mountains leaving their great sides bare. The river, or Sound, lets the fog in from the sea, and it passes away northward, clearing our position entirely from its presence.

Towards sunset Louisa and I strolled out on the S.W. Harbor road; and returned with a profusion of wintergreen blossoms.

The aspect of the west was remarkable. A range of dense clouds rearing their heads above the horizon, with a background of clear sky, moved solemnly towards the north, wearing the aspect of a grand procession of animals. Here were wild oxen three abreast, with horns spreading, and projecting tails; then a group of camels with burdens; in another point a crowd of elephants; and as the procession pressed along new goblins arose, men and birds and rocks. All were in a grand scale, and the resemblances were startling. This lasted some minutes, and not only gratified us intensely, but suggested the deeper horrors which might be excited in the superstitious by such a scene. With a large experience of watching clouds, and a proneness to imagine something more than their forms image, I never saw half so fine a pictorial show of clouds. Meantime the region above acquired a vast scarlet band, turning to purple, which stretched over it like a drawn up curtain. *

The lady fishermen came home with a basket of mackerel; the party have taken 60 of that sort, and some 20 fish of other kinds. *

Today Mr. Winthrop opened his poetry upon us again with the following lines; which were received with great pleasure.

Mr. Winthrop's Verses

"Droop lower gloom! and hide
Years that are gone, and years that are to be.
This urgent future like a tide
Whelms my vain struggling with eternity.
Wrap closer, mists! Not one

Of my fair, fluttering, comrade hopes is nigh;
Their white sails faded with the sun
And I drift where I lost them, cheerlessly."

Thus mused I; when a gush
Of girlish laughter danced along the air;
Voices as radiant as a flush
Of sunbeams, that the ripples cannot bear.

To sea and smile not — sounds
Of finest graceful gladness, such as wake
Givers of joy throbs, stronger bounds
All upward pulsing, till our stirred hearts take

One leaf to ecstasy;
And poising, as an eaglet on a breeze,
Are fanned to realms of fantasy
Heavenward sweeping over sparkling seas;

Then droops in pensive peace.
Oh that soft melody! My gloom is fled.
Never may that fresh laughter cease;
Or live in echoes circling overhead

As faint gold halos crown
The saintliness of maidens, only seen,
When full of starlight, eyes glance down
And recognize on earth a sister sheen.

Saturday. August 18. 1855.

This day I proposed to spend with Fanny and Clara on foot, between here and Southwest Harbor. It was steamer day there, and we expected Mr. Howard's party and Mr. Fay had some hopes of other arrivals. We started off, and walked through in two hours and three minutes - (seven miles)- and met the passengers leaving the boat. None of our friends came. We lounged on the wharf and saw "David" load his sailboat with two families and their luggage, and set sail for Northeast Harbor, with a "smart" wind. Then going up to Clark's "Island House," we waited for our dinner. The waggon came down while we waited, and the persons in it were as much disappointed as we. They went home to dine at three o'clock, but my young pedestrians refused seats in the waggon. Mr. Clark's good dinner, and a quiet lounge, made them ready for return. A gentleman, just arrived, gave us a Boston paper of yesterday, and the last Punch. I suspect his name is Piston but am not sure. He is a thorough Oriental in his language, and colossal & superb in his person.

We groped home, being in no hurry. The drinking cup of birch bark, made in the morning walk, served us for draughts from many springs. Choosing a pretty spot in the woods, about half way, we made a resting place on a shawl, and I proceeded to basket making while the girls were hunting for pigeon berries and fruits & flowers. The pin in my cravat served as a needle, and a small parcel of cotton thread from Fanny's pocket furnished the sewing twine, with which I made two white birch bark baskets, large & strong enough for their uses. One of them we filled with red raspberries for Annie, and the other with wintergreen blossoms for decorations. We made no haste, but fulfilled the 14 miles walk at sunset, bringing our baskets, and shawl, and an umbrella, and a store of choice birch bark.

There we found that the boys who had gone out in the waggon with the young ladies & gentlemen, had been sent home with the waggon from Beech Hill, and the party intended to ascend a mountain there and return on foot.

Tea time came, & no return. 9 o'clock came, and Mrs. Fay began to be anxious. The party consisted of 5 young ladies – Miss Fay, 2

Misses Church & Cordelia & Mary; and Mr. Church, Mr. Winthrop, James Fay & Kent Stone. I slipped out quietly and went up to the second ascent on the road leading towards Beech Hill, and listened for their approach. All was silent. I shouted. They knew my shout before. The voice came back in five different echoes, and must have penetrated a long distance. No answer. I waited, and shouted repeatedly, with the same result. At eleven o'clock it seemed best to know more about the party, for fear some misfortune had befallen them. They were without thick shawls, or provisions, and might suffer from the cold of the night if lost or disabled. Mr. Green was dispatched to Beech Hill to make discoveries. About midnight he returned, having gone to the spot where they dismissed the waggon, and found they had not been heard of since.

Mrs. Fay's anxiety was extreme. Speculation could do little in such a case. But it was possible they had gone over the mountain towards Southwest Harbor, & might be found there, or that they had encamped on the slope of the mountain. So Mr. Green and I took a fresh start, and we both went to S.W. Harbor, shouting occasionally, and constantly listening and looking. The night was calm, and stars shining behind the hill tops would often mislead us. But there were no visible fires, & no answers to our shouts, but the most reverberant echoes.

Getting beyond Dennin's Pond, we roused Mr. Lurvey, as his house was the first on that side of the forest, but he had heard nothing.

Just as we were on the point of reaching Clark's, I encountered my mishap — simply a sprained knee — by an accident with the waggon. No news of the party there.

Fortunately for our expedition, the accident took place in front of Mr. Freeman's house, and he is the blacksmith. He was aroused & made the needful repairs while Green went in & consulted with Clark. The result was that the party had not been heard of, and it must be they had camped out for the night. Freeman thought they might be trapped on a mountain there which can only be ascended or descended at one point; and some cattle, having strayed there, could not get down at all and came near dying of hunger.

Returning home we shouted & watched, but had no answer, and

saw no light. The dawn began as we came up, and the causes of anxiety were certainly drawing to a close.

Mr. Green then harnessed the great waggon, and went down to bring home the party, with an abundance of shawls and coats.

Soon after sunrise of Sunday morning Mr. Church came in on foot, and reported that all was right; and long before breakfast time the waggon brought all the party home safe and bright.

Mr. Church had led them to the head of Crescent Lake, and up the mountain — the 3rd from the sound — or the next west of the Western Mountain.[41] The ascent proved difficult, the party moved slow, and when it was half way up the sun set & growing darkness compelled them to return. Coming down as well as they might, they reached the base in a thick wood, in total darkness, and without a path. Mr. Church then managed to guide them down to the shore of the lake, and along it till they reached a fair broad beach. He then raised a fire, by matches from his pocket, and they soon were sitting in a happy state around a huge roaring fire of drift wood and evergreen boughs. The gentlemen then prepared a bed for the ladies, — of green boughs — and put them together, covered them over with shawls, and let them sleep till morning. By broad daylight, they all left this camp, and reaching a farmer's house found some bread and milk before our waggon arrived. They all declared they had a capital time and that the conduct and skill of the gentlemen was admirable.[42]

Mr. Church, by the campfire light, made sketches of the group sitting about the fire, and of the "Babes in the Woods" as the ladies slept.

Cordelia's birthday came at midnight, and she then received the usual greetings, before they went to their rest.

Sunday. Augt. 19. 1855.

My injury kept me still all day. The wood party slept most of the day. The younger of the party went to church and heard the Methodist minister.

Annie was so sick as to keep Louisa pretty busy all day.

My drowsiness and the prescription to lie still kept me from all occupations.

In the evening all were bright, and we had psalmody in great perfection.

Monday. Augt. 20. 1855.

My experience today has been within doors. The children have fished, and they brought home about two dozen mackerel.

A party has driven to Indian Point. The mail has brought us quantities of letters and papers. Another party has taken a sail in the harbor, and saw a live seal in the water.

One great piece of news, is by Mr. Titus' letter, in which he informs me of his coming this present week with his two eldest daughters to join our party.

My friend (Piston?#) called today, to inquire after the party and after me. We entertained him with the sketches and the stories; and gave him some apples from our stores.

In the evening we had charades — the words being portrait (pour & trate) and pollock (poll-luck). The imitations were most capital, and the whole effect fine.

This was the test day of Annie's fever, and the chill did not come. I breathe more freely.

I subsequently learned his true name to be Porter; and I had his professional card as a lawyer in Boston.

Tuesday. August 21. 1855.

Great preparations were on foot for an early start of a party for Schooner Head. The result was that not much before ten o'clock, the start was complete. Mr. Church and his two sisters, Miss Fay, Cordelia & Mary, and James Fay & Kent Stone, in the waggon, and Mr. Winthrop on horse back, made up the load. They are to drive directly to Lynams, take luncheon there, & spend the afternoon viewing the sights, and come home seasonably this evening.

I have staid[43] about the house all day. Louisa and the littlest girls are walking this afternoon to the lakes. Charlie and Clem, have been bathing. Fanny, Clara, and Arthur have been rambling up the mill brook, & gathering flowers. Miss Fay is not well, and stays in her room.

Annie is decidedly better. Her tongue is clear, she has appetite, sits up, feels well, and mends.

The air is most delicious and the prospect from the house is in the most perfect light. It grows brighter & more beautiful day by day, and if Annie can get out to enjoy it again while it is so lovely I shall be perfectly happy.

My capacity for basket making, and general chipping in birch bark, is bringing me into business. The little girls are calling for all sorts of articles.

The Schooner Head party returned in great spirits.

Wednesday. Augt. 22. 1855.

A fine day. Two waggons drove to Southwest Harbor to meet the Steam Boat. I found a seat in the waggon did me no harm and so went. Mr. Fay returned, and brought with him Mr. Robert S. Littell who joins our party.

This morning I was induced to recite my lines "To the Ocean*" written twenty years ago, and recollected with difficulty & not perfectly. The company listened, but I don't know whether they admired.

This afternoon I lounged, and this evening sat with the party in the parlor.

Annie has had a slight chill today, and goes to bed dosed with quinine.

* See post [end pages 140-142.]

Thursday. Augt. 23. 1855.

A cloudy, foggy, showery day. In the morning I went out with two boat parties, & we caught 53 Mackerel, and saw several huge eagles. In the meantime invitations were prepared at the house, as from the boarders, to sundry people and families in the village for next Tuesday evening at 6 1/2 o'clock. Mr. Winthrop has been out the whole morning to find a bird for Annie, but without any success. It was so kind of him, and he did not even find a robbin while he got drenched with rain.

Annie has gone down stairs, to sit at the dinner table: - the first time for many days. It is refreshing to have her approach herself again.

Friday. Augt. 24. 1855.

(My journalizing has fallen in arrears while the illness of Annie and my own slight lameness have kept me from going conveniently to my room. I resume it from this date, after six days interruption — August 30th.)

Today we drove to Schooner Head. I scrambled over the rocks to the Devil's Oven,[44] a deep cavern on the bluff water front. The ocean beats directly into it, and the huge cell, about 75 feet from front to rear, must roar terrifically when the tide reaches into it. Big Head[45] is a grand lookout point. I stopped there to rest my knee, while the party rambled further.

This tramp cost me some pains, but it paid very well. The Sea was blue and the horizon clear, and the wide plain was specked with shipping. We saw a pair of pigeons near the road which would not fly for our shouting — the gun of course was left at home.

Nancy Jane was actually at home, and I saw her. She is a myth no longer, but a grand reality; - a girl of 17 years and about 1 7/8 yards high, fair, with red cheeks & lips, flaxen haired, and well formed, and withal pretty. I should have taken her for a remarkably fine specimen of the German damsels.

Schooner Head has its name from the appearance of white spots and veins in the rocky front, in the form of a Schooner. It is said that a

British ship of war, in a foggy time, fired into the Schooner several times before discovering that it was shot proof. From Big Head I could see a part of the white marks, appreciated the naming as well deserved.

This time we came home early.

Saturday. Augt. 25. 1855.

The waggon went down today and brought up our friends Mr. Titus and his daughters, Lucretia and Annie, most welcome & happy accessions to our party.

In the afternoon we sent them off to Beech Hill, to see the lakes. Their time being short, we push them about rapidly.

The invitations for our party have gone forth. It seems that at first the people thought we were trying to get them here & make fun of them for our amusement. Some better advice has prevailed, and we now expect a good turnout.

The preparations go on steadily & formidably. Jellies & custards & whips are ripening up, and there are nuts & figs and sugar plums, & apples & pears, and there will be lobster salad.

I rowed a boat this afternoon, and think myself getting on better.

Sunday. August 26. 1855.

We went in a body to the church and heard Mr. Bowker, twice. His two sermons were remarkably good. The last was his valedictory; and it was well conceived and well expressed. We are always pleased with the substantial, respectable & devout appearance of this congregation. They are making a manifest effort to produce good choir singing; but their selection of tunes is out of some new collection, & the result is not musical. They have once sung an old tune, and we all joined in it.

I have finished Laborde,[46] and read much in the Review:

Laborde is evidently a sincere writer and a true Christian, although deeply tinged with the errors of his church. I think of him with great kindness, and not without hope of his yet emerging from the dark places of superstition.

Monday. Augt. 27. 1855.

This day deprives us of a part of our original company. Mr. Fay, with his whole family (excepting Miss Fay) and Jas. Kent Stone, go home together.[47] Their stay has been so pleasant to them and to us, that the parting has a touch of sadness. Miss Fay is left in my party, to go with us to Boston next week.

Mr. Somes offered to take some of us down in his sail boat, by which he goes to the custom house at Southwest Harbor. Mr. Titus, the two Misses Titus, Mr. Littell, Fanny and Charlie & I took seats in his boat. The wind was dead astern, and we skimmed over the water in gay style. Mr. Somes pointed out the landmarks. There is one small isolated mountain which is called the flying mountain; the Indian tradition being that this place flew off from the larger mountain next it, & alighted in the sound. A firm smooth precipice on one shore is called dog mountain;[48] because there a dog was thrown off many years ago, when two ladies were roaming over the cliff.

At the landing we found our waggon load in readiness awaiting the arrival of the Steamer. Our approach was across the point on foot, the wind requiring us to land on the windward side. Our landing was rather scattering, as the wind was brisk. The gentlemen helped as they could, and I saw at one time a pair of heels in the air, and a pair of spectacles flying over the water. No bones being broken, we came off in grand spirits.

The steamer came in time, & we parted from our friends, with rather a sober farewell, & came home to Somesville.

In the afternoon Louisa went with a party to show the Notch and Notch Lake to the Tituses.

While they were out Charlie & I went out & shot some birds for Annie, who can now eat of such treat, but not of the usual fish diet.

In the evening we had a concert of music, and some games.

The night came off cold & clear, and there was a frost in the morning of the 28th.

Tuesday. Augt. 28. 1855. Frosty morning.

This day the party that is to be is sending shadows over the house. Louisa and Mr. Church stay in all day to make the preparations. The waggon is sent to Schooner Head for the Lynams.

In the morning Mr.Titus and Mr. Littell, with a party, go to Newport Mountain, and I go along to stop at Eagle Lake; Mr. Dodge (our Charioteer) and I intending to catch trout while the party are on the mountain.

Unfortunately, the boat had sunk, and it would be a day's work to get her up & in order for use. Dodge and I therefore lounged at the lake, ate bread & milk at Newman's,[49] and I strolled home on foot, taking many rests on the way, and so using up the afternoon.

The invitations are for 6 1/2 p.m. Guests were here from Southwest Harbor, Bar Harbor & Schooner head, and the posse of Somesville.[50] The dining room was cleared, and made our third saloon, all gaily lighted up. A fiddler and fluteplayer were stationed at the end of the long room, and dancing went on there while conversation had full course in the two parlors. The chief piece of light fixture was a candelabra made of a young pine tree top, with many branches, all trimmed with green & cranberries and vines. It bore 14 candles, and as we were supplied with spermaceti [51] and stearin candles from New York, the illumination was brilliant. The whole party numbered 80 persons, including ourselves. Of course they were all strangers to us, but we made ourselves very easy, & soon all the houseful was in a state of sociability & happiness. Early coffee and tea warmed up the party. The dance helped. The piano was always going, & we had songs & glees [52] in abundance. Later in the evening the supper table was ready, & with marching music we promenaded the company into the supper room. Mr. Winthrop had prepared a delicious lobster salad, and Mr. Church had cut out vegetable flowers to ornament the dishes.[53] The soft custard, the snowy capped whipped cream, the fruits arranged for effect, the chandelier, the jellies, the cakes, and the et ceteras, made a really pretty table. When it had been duly admired, we fell to. The side tables gave duck and sandwiches; and so we made out a various feast. Nothing could surpass the popularity of the entertainment. The evening flew off after this, at a grand rate. The table was cleared, & the dance resumed. The company gradually dropped away from 12 to 1 o'clock, and finally at 2 a.m. the last guests, the two Miss Roberts [54] of Bar Harbor, drove away alone by moonlight. We offered them a bed, but they would not stay; and to our admiration they drove their own waggon. To ensure them against the cold, we wrapped the two together under my large maud [55]: and we saw them drive off bravely. They took the old road, which is 14 miles long, and reached home in two hours. We saw them the next day. They had accomplished the journey without harm, and put up their own horse in the barn before retiring to the house.

The whole affair was successful in the best sense.[56] It gave real pleasure to all our guests, and more or less to all of us. The young ladies — whose names generally are Somes, or Noyes, or Thomas, were very pretty, and bore the marks of refinement of feeling, and something of the practice of usages of society. Mr. Winthrop improvised verses for the soup, bringing in the wonders of this island, and the whole company seemed to appreciate the wit & fun of his performance.

Wednesday. August 29. 1855.

Schooner Head again. This time we had three waggons. The day was perfectly fine. We had a grand time. This spot grows on us. Mr. Winthrop went to the top of the precipice, 1200 ft. high, and described the Ocean view as the finest he has yet found. Charlie & I strolled about Schooner Head & the Cove, watching the breakers, while the others went to the Ovens and the shell beach. The waves which break on these rocks come up in full force to the very shore and thunder against the jagged rocks. For a long distance there is no beach at all, but the waves break square upon the wall of rock. The crests and the wide spaces sparkling with foam are superb.

*The brown bread & rich milk we obtained here were a feast for us, and everyone indulged freely.

As I was driving home on a seat with Fanny, the two Miss Tituses being on the back seat, we met with a funny accident. The irons of the front seat failed instantly and Fanny & I were down. No serious damage was done to us, but the seat was incurable. I therefore placed the seat and cushion & my shawl so that the two, Annie and Fanny, sat facing backwards, vis a vis to Lucretia & me who were on the back seat, and so we drove to Eagle Lake. The whole affair went off as a frolick & joke, and the young ladies were hardly persuaded to quit their comical seat and take the places open for them in the large waggon.

The evening was enlivened with a very funny charade: "perpetual," and then the company were driven off to their rest. *

Thursday. Augt. 30. 1855.

This morning we have parted with Mr. Titus and his daughters, and with Mr. Winthrop. The little time the Tituses have been with us has been used in the most active pursuit of sightseeing. They have given us great pleasure, and profess to have taken much themselves. Mr. Winthrop has been invaluable. He is full of all sorts of capacities for such a life as we lead here, and has ministered to everybody's gratification. He came to stay one week, and has staid three; and he says he never had so pleasant a three weeks in his life.

His versification powers have been put in requisition to good effect.

Among other things he produced, and gave to Mary, the following:

By Mr. Winthrop

The Dreamy Sea

Oh let me look upon that dreamy sea!
A wild love -longing for its mystery
Has mastered, ever thrills and masters me.
My soul sweeps outward to the infinite,
Trembling along the delicate delight
Of waves that brighten on, and on, and run
To fade in mist that is all sea and sun.

~

Oh let me gaze upon that dreamy sea!
It sends such quivering looks, so smilingly
Answers my smile, that its broad majesty
But deepens joy - else it might break and waste
On gay and dimpled laughter, that has chased
Away the nobleness of silence. Now
These smilecrests fitly gem this royal brow.

~

Oh let me look upon that dreamy sea!
Life has not crushed & dwarfed me utterly.
All furled and drooping though the sails may be.
Let the great winds but strike them, they will bear
Much baffling yet, so but the pilot dare
To plunge. Down twilight, drift this darkness on,
Till some vast summer wave is red with dawn.

~

Oh let me dream beside this dreamy sea!
Ever and ever falling soothingly,
Ripples are pleading with their melody:
The massy breakers cast their might away:
And fringing sea-weeds flicker in the sway
Of wavering waters, as a maidens hair
Is caught and fondled by the summer air.

~

The voices in the surges speak to me
Of struggles and endurance, and a free
Dash at the fates that front us terribly:
For we are flung on life as on a surge,

Heaved along unknown currents, till we merge
Our being into vastness — then we cease
Yielding and borne down steadier flow of peace,

~

But peace of grander action. — Dreamily
Then let me look beyond this dim, dim sea!
Our dreams but shadow what our lives may be.
Hopes are more real than all that hopes achieve.
Visions — oh nobler than we dare believe!
Suddenly will burst on us of glorious lands
And glorious oceans foaming up their strands.

During this forenoon, Mr. Littell & Clara went out with the row boat & fishing tackle. We heard nothing from them and the wind blew off shore tremendously. At dinner table their places were vacant. After dinner, and as late as 3 1/2 p.m., they came in sight near Crane Point, and were seen rowing, each with an oar, along the shore, so as to reach our cove by a line less affected with the roll of the water. It had grown calmer, but the pulling was evidently hard. I watched them, & made them see my handkerchief, and they came on tugging hard. When they came to land Clara's hair was out at length, her face pale with the effort and anxiety, her feet numb with cold, & Mr. Littell thoroughly tired & wet. They went out with a favoring wind, crossed the bar, dropped anchor & proceeded to fishing. Shortly afterwards they discovered that the boat had dragged her anchor, and while they deemed her motion due merely to waves she had gone about two miles below the island & was drifting very fast. They both took to the oars, and made for the home shore. Their course lay through the trough of the sea, and they were put to their utmost power to reach the shore. Then they were far down below the point, and the wind was ahead. More than once Mr. Littell had to go on shore and drag the boat around a point. The whole affair was trying to both, and showed that they were "game."

This afternoon Annie was taken out to ride in the great waggon. We went to Beech Hill and stopped at a house for Annie, and when she was rested returned. The ride did her good; and it shows that our present plan is advisable; namely to take her to Lynam's next Monday & keep her there till well enough to go home. She found the air at Lynam's the most refreshing of any point on the island. It comes either from the mountain, or the forest, or the blue ocean without a margin of muddy beach. It must be curative. Louisa will go with her when the rest of my party start for home. Mr. Church and one or both of his sisters will go with them & stay while they stay.

This evening our circle has been more quiet, but not lacking in agreeable occupations.

A good fire of wood has been the center of attraction within. The moonlight rowing parties are better for warmer weather.

Friday. Augt. 31. 1855.

We set out at noon, a party of eleven, with two waggons, and pursued the North East Harbor road. Passing the Notch Lake, we rolled down the winding wood road to the harbor, thence along the shore and around on the rough road that skirts the ocean along the south shore of the island. The aspect of the island from this route is exceedingly wild & frowning. The mountains are sharp, bare & ragged, and the calm, wide blue ocean on the other side stretches a long, long horizon, only marked with scattering sails. The road is hilly, rocky, & almost impassable. We walked most of the distance. Now it was up & down a rocky back of ground, with a sweeping view on all sides, and now down through a ravine or cove where we struck tidewater and forded, or crossed on bridges, the water way through a sand or gravel bar against which the sea was rolling in. Once we mistook our route, and went wrong a long mile up hill; & on finding the end of a road we also discovered a dark lake walled in with precipitous mountains. The farthest boundary of the lake was beneath a pair of hills, so exactly alike, & yet so well rounded & hemispherical, that we named them the Twin Hills, and the lake Twinhill Pond.[57]

After completing 15 miles of jaunting, in 5 hours time, we stopped at a small farm house on Otter Creek, and made our repast, partly from our own basket & partly from provisions found by the family. The house was upon a hill looking over the land into the ocean. The farmer, Mr. Smallage, was an old man, native of the island, who came to this spot 20 years ago and cleared this farm from its native forest. His crop consists chiefly of fire wood which is sent to Boston. Mrs. Smallage was a stout old woman, a snuff taker. The married daughter (Mrs. Tracy) and a very pretty daughter of 15 made up the party. The girl was one of the prettiest we have met on the island; which is saying much after the show of fair ones at our party.

We crowded around a little table, and had a feast of the most ravenous and cheery sort. The family seemed to wonder at and enjoy our pleasure in an extraordinary manner.

The horses have taken oats while we took ham, eggs, bread, milk, cranberries, pies, chocolate, tea, cake & other things, we set out at 6 o'clock and drove down into the grand notch between the precipice-mountain at Lynams and the next mountain west of it.[58] As we went on, the notch formed splendidly around as we descended lower at every step and the crags on each side drew up higher as we went, until we reached a narrow flat or bottom, where the two mountains stand up on either side & stretch on a mile or more without retreating or falling off. The mountains there are not perpendicular, but very steep, & yield barely earth enough to sustain the scattering growth of gnarled pines, which as we looked upward appeared somewhat like an orchard.

The interest of this day was great; and so far as the mountain & ocean scenery is concerned, we deemed the drive a fine termination of our rambles.

At evening we drew up at Bar Harbor; and the horses having drawn us 20 miles over mountain roads were given their rest.

Mr. Roberts' tavern amply accommodated the party, and by ten o'clock they were distributed in their rooms.

The circle drawn up around the wood fire before retiring demanded stories; and so Mr. Church and I were drawn upon for story telling. I gave them the old Oneida tale of Staring, and the other of the baby loaned to the indians.

Saturday. Sept. 1. 1855.

At 6 we were roused; at 6 1/2 we took our seats at the breakfast table.

The drive back to Somesville was by the old road [59] (so called) 14 miles i.e., 6 miles further than our usual route. This took us along the shore of Frenchmans Bay, by a very good road, and among farms nearly the whole distance. There is no end of schoolhouses on this island, and the imagination is exerted to find children back on these green wood lanes to supply the buildings with scholars. Churches, of various sizes and pretensions, are abundant also. We argue very well of the character of the people from this decided and general attention to the external conveniences of learning and religion.

The packing up is going forward briskly today. The plan is to evacuate Somesville Monday; all going home except Mrs. Tracy & Annie, and Mr. Church & one of his sisters, and they four go to Lynams till Annie is better able to go home, or till the weather in New York shall be fit for her return. The piano is to go back to Boston by a schooner.

Sunday. Sept. 2. 1855.

No service in the church today. We led a quiet life in the house. During the forenoon a party from Milton arrived, part by waggon and part by a boat, from Souwest harbor; and after dinner they went on to Roberts at Bar Harbor for a few days stay. The ladies appeared like superior persons; but I was willing to let the party go by with their slack notions of Sunday keeping, although we with just hospitality provided them rooms in our quarters if they would stay here.

In the afternoon Louisa and I walked out to Beech Hill, and called at the house of Mr. Richardson where Annie had her rest a few days ago. Four men, now old, were born on the farm, and jointly inherited its 150 acres from their father. They divided it up, and each built on his fourth part; and they are here spending old age in the same place. The utmost simplicity, kindness, and contentment seems to mark this little colony.

A superb sunset shone over us as we came home.

This evening we had psalmody, the last music we may expect in this party; and I closed the piano with as good an opinion of its tone and its good offices as ever was due to a musical instrument.

Monday. Sept. 3. 1855.

Off for home. Mr. Somes took two in his waggon. Dodge took all the rest. Mr. Church going on the steps. A neighboring waggon was chartered for the baggage.

We took leave of the house and the family, and of Louisa, Annie, and Miss Church; a parting cheerful in the main, but crossed with some shadows of sadness.

Driving to Souwest Harbor we had songs and glees from the young ladies, and took one last echo from the Dennins Pond precipice. *

At Roberts[60] we waited long for the Boat; and bade good bye to Mr. Dodge our charioteer — a very sensible, well mannered, kind, pleasant fellow, who parted from us with a expression of sadness on his countenance which did him real credit.

At length the boat came just as we were attacking Mr. Clark's bread, milk & pie. We ran off with bits in our hands and made a very swift chase for the dock, reaching it barely in time to save our passage. The *Rockland* swept around the harbor, and we signaled Mr. Church till white handkerchiefs grew invisible.

Mt. Desert Island, as we left it, seemed vastly more imposing than ever before. It was a clear day; the sun was in the right point; and the sea as calm as a lake. Those grand, rough, jagged, independent looking mountains, reaching so far away, and seeming to rise out of the waves, have no equals in interest on the whole coast, if anywhere else. The passage to Rockland, among the islands, is much like the sail down the Thousand Isles of the St. Lawrence; and equally interesting. Our party kept on the upper deck all day, refusing dinner, but baiting from a large basket of sundries, and the ladies felt so gay as actually to sing and dance on the deck. A wandering fiddler thereupon proposed to fiddle for a general dance on the deck; whereupon the young ladies gave over the fancy to dance there and the performance closed.

As we crossed the Penobscot Bay, we came in sight of the steamer *Penobscot*, hurrying into port from the river a little before us. Our staterooms were engaged and paid for in her, and we now heard that the *Rockland* sometimes misses her, and then the passengers take the *Boston* and have berths after herds of cattle and sheep. Our anxieties however were brief, for we reached our berth five minutes after the *Penobscot*; and bag and baggage, with owners and keepers, went safely into the grand sea steamer: we then for the first time touching the main-land of Maine, by crossing over the wharf on foot.

On the *Penobscot* we found our staterooms duly reserved, and took possession at once. In half an hour tea was ready, and our party was the first to reach the table, and about the last to leave it. Such a feast and such a hungry company rarely meet.

The boat had nearly seven hundred passengers and a ships company of about sixty-five, making over 700 souls on board. The discharge of a campmeeting up the river, helped to swell the number. People stretched themselves everywhere, and we had hard way to come at our rooms.

During the afternoon after tea and the evening, we sat on the stern deck, and had a rare time. The sunset was most brilliant. The forms and colors were remarkably rich, and lasted long, while the opposite heavens, at the sea horizon, presented a superb counterpart. As it grew darker, the phosphorescent insects in the sea began to flash out and during the whole evening the path of the vessel was resplendent with these starry lights. It is singular that this is the first time I ever saw such a sight, or any of the sea lights of which I have always heard so much; and yet I have been back & forth occasionally on salt water all my life.

When it grew quite dark, the crowd on the stern deck began to grow musical. Our party sang some glees, and a larger party, near but not distinguishable by the eye, sang several Virginia airs. At last, as the singers grew interested, both parties sang together and produced a grand vocal concert of glees & negro melodies. It was a wild, democratic, free & easy, sort of affair; but it was done cheerily and in the true passion for music; and I thought it no small sign of the growing musical furor of the country, and of the efficient instrumentality of the Ethiopian Minstrelsy in working the revolution.

The sea was charmingly quiet; and when out on the ocean beyond all sight of shore, there was no roll which could disturb the most inexperienced of landsmen.

Tuesday. Sept. 4. 1855.

All hands were mustered early, and from the decks we saw the island and the city as the boat entered Boston Harbor.

At the dock we met Mr. Fay & Arthur. Everything was found, and off we went to the railroad station. There we breakfasted in the refreshment room, and made ready for the express train. Miss Fay & Mr. Littell, here parted from us for Brookline.

The day was fine. We flew along through the beautiful village and farmfield scenes of Massachusetts. At Springfield we met the Misses Tituses at the station, and saw them five minutes.

At Hartford we landed Miss C. Church in safety; and being reduced to our family party, including Cordelia Kirkland, we glided on.

At 5 p.m. we were in our own house, and all sound and well; not having entered a house since we started, and having travelled 450 miles in 30 hours without serious fatigue. The house is in fine order, and the children are overwhelmed at its size & the height of the ceilings, after so long bending under tapering walls and jostling in narrow rooms. The yard excites our wonder. The vines have grown wildly for 36 days, and have covered the fences & hung festoons all around our premises. The flowers are richly blossoming. The little party feel as if they had fallen into an enchanted spot.

Thus ends an expedition which has been interesting, instructive, and often exciting, in a very high degree. It will be the fund of story

& conversation, for years to come. The children come back, broader, and browner, and stronger, than they went.

By a letter subsequently received, I find that Louisa took Annie safely to Schooner Head yesterday, and the party of four are now there, and that Annie was feeling better this morning & proposing a walk after breakfast. This news came Saturday morning Sept. 8th, and gratified us much.

Still later, on the 14th of September, they reached home, having highly enjoyed the visit at Schooner Head, & made the journey home by another route than ours. They were rowed by Mr. Lynam 16 miles, to the mainland, & thence drove in waggons to Bucksport. Thence by the inside passage to Portland, & thence by railroad. They passed nights at Bucksport, Boston & Hartford, and left the Churches at their home in Hartford.

Annie has become almost restored. Schooner Head has done much for her.

So it all ends well.

Mount Desert Island had its name from the French. The inhabitants pronounce it Mount De-sert' (accent on final syllable). There was nothing like barrenness or desert condition about the island in those days. The mountains were clothed with large timber within half a century past, and have only since that time become bare rocks by the burning of the forests. The huge trunks of the old woods stand and lie, bleached white, around the slopes of the bare mountains, in proof of the recentness of the old forests. The better impression is that the French saw the mountains, looking like one grand mountain when approached from the east, and then missed it in the fogs, its form thus deserting them. They said it deserts us, and hence named the mountains Mount Desert!

If the New Englanders had named the place, the word Mount would be prolonged to Mountain, and would be made to follow, not precede, the other term. It would have been Desert Mountain, not Mount Desert.

The French had a small settlement at the point near Southwest Harbor, but no traces of it remain now.

This island is about 15 miles in diameter, and is not far from circular in its general outline. On the northwest side it lies near the main land, so that the road crosses by a bridge. The northeasterly parts look into Frenchmans Bay, and have a line of cultivated farms. The southwesterly part is along the narrow bays which the island-bearing coast of Maine abounds in, being of all forms and sizes. The southeasterly side, reaching almost half around the island, fronts the Ocean, with the free sea and unbroken water horizon. The island surface may be divided into two semi-circles; one of which, next the Ocean, is occupied with the range of mountains, and the other with rolling land. The mountains rise up near the shore, & their bases only reach back to the central region of the island. They are, (generally described), a range of independent mountains separated by deep gorges which run towards the ocean. In one gorge there is the Sound — Somes Sound — a mile wide and seven miles long, overhung by steeps like the roughest Highlands of the Hudson. In others there are long deep lakes, in others narrow notches with wild precipices at the sides. The lakes are numerous — some say 15 in number. I have visited nine of them, one 6 miles long, two of 3 miles each, and others of considerable size.

The farming is peculiar. Along Frenchman Bay the land seemed to be more fully cultivated, but most of the island is used for cutting wood for the Boston market, or for grazing a few cattle and sheep. The men are much drawn away on the sea as sailors or fishermen, and hence the cultivation about a farmhouse is generally limited to the production of hay for use on the premises, and a small patch of oats, buckwheat, corn, barley, and potatoes, & sometimes of wheat, for the supply of the establishment. At almost every house there are racks standing in the yard for curing fish, and the curing, or "making," of codfish is always going on.

The inhabitants seem to be in a comfortable state between riches and poverty, none hitting either extreme. On Sundays the fisheries cease, and a well dressed population turns out to church. Meeting houses and schoolhouses are everywhere. The dialect and tone is New Englandish, but much less provincial than the conversational language of some parts further west. We were hospitably and considerately treated and received wherever we went, and never encountered any offensive or prying inquisitiveness.

*To the Ocean.**

Composed under the influence of my first visit to the shore. It was at Long Branch, twenty years ago the present month of August. So I endeavored to recall and recite the stanzas. I now write them out, as germain to the Log Book.

Thou mightiest work of nature's hand,
Deep, spacious, rolling sea:
Art thou the offspring of the land,
The oozings of the lea?
Or wast thou ere the dawn of light,
And didst heave up the ground,
And dash the towering mountain height

With shells from thy profound?

~

When natal hymns to Earth were sung
With chorus of the spheres,
When Heaven with joyous shouting rung
Join'dst thou the morning stars?
Peal'dst thou thy deep toned organ voice,
As now in pride thou dost,
With heaving bosom didst rejoice
To embrace the new born coast?

~

Forever roll, thou mighty deep!
Thy waves shall sink and rise,
And pulse of life for nature keep,
Till perish earth and skies.
Thy gifts shall feed, thy breath shall fan,
Thy powerful hand uphold
The myriads of future man,
Until his race is told.

~

If thy great Author were not known
By revelation clear,
I'd worship thee — and thee alone —
A god without a peer.
Amid the sparkling surf should stand
My altar reared to thee,
I'd offer there rich golden sand
And gems of brilliancy.

~

My song should swell in lofty strain
Along thy breakers crest,
While thine own music shook the main
Thy favor to attest.
I'd worship thee as born ere birth,
To live till nought should be,—

The throbbing heart of living earth —
Thy self Eternity.

~

The many to the sun might bow,
And build pagodas tall,
And burning incense, might avow
He was the god o'er all;
But I would stroll the lonely beach
And wet me in thy spray: —
Sublimer lessons thou canst teach
Than can the King of Day.

~

Thy waters, ever pure, defy
Corruptions every form,
And thou diffusest purity
E'en in thy raging storm.
What image hath gross earth like thee
Of heavens exalted King,
Whose face the pure alone shall see,
Whose praise they only sing.

~

Adieu, thou most of all sublime!
Old Ocean fare thee well.
I seek again the interior clime,
The grove, the lake, the dell.
Thy god like voice, thy living face,
Thy deep eternal roll, —
Thy wonders all - will I retrace,
For aye, with thrilled soul.

*[*See reference to this poem in body of text, p. 123]*

Portraits

Members of the Party

Louisa Kirkland Tracy

Charles Tracy

Painted by Daniel Huntington
circa 1860s

Frances Tracy c. 1855-60

Annie Tracy c. 1860

Charlic Tracy c. 1855

Frederic Edwin Church
1860

Theodore Winthrop
1861

James Harrison Fay
Age about 21 years

Rev. John Seeley Stone
Age about 70 years

James Kent Stone
Age about 19 years

Afterword

Further biographical information and what happened later in the lives of the members of the party.

The Tracy Family

Charles Tracy handled litigation for the railroads in his own firm of Tracy, Olmstead & Tracy. He was also legal advisor to J. Pierpont Morgan, his son-in-law, and his friend, the artist, Frederic Edwin Church. At the time of the diary, he lived near St. George's Church, where he later came to know J. Pierpont Morgan, and where his daughter Frances was married to Morgan. Tracy was vestryman and warden of that church. A memorial building to both Charles and **Louisa** Tracy was donated to the church by the Morgans. Tracy bought an old apple farm on the Hudson River, near West Point, where his descendants still live. The diary makes several comparisons between the mountains on Mount Desert Island and the Hudson River landscape; such as Butter Hill, now Storm King.

Annie did recover from the lingering illness which Tracy talks about with such feeling in the diary. She is mentioned in Adelma Joy's account of that summer as the young lady who never went about with the party, but preferred to wander through the village with her little sister (Julia) in tow.[1] However, her adult life was brief and ill-fated. She married Lindley Miller in 1862. He was a combatant in the Civil War when she gave birth to her first child at the time of the Draft Riots in New York. It was during the three-day period of riots, when Negroes were being hunted down mercilessly and murdered by an angry mob, that Tracy, an abolitionist and Republican supporter of the Civil War, helped his son-in-law to rescue his Negroe servants. At the time, he blamed the Irish working class for the upheaval. Annie died of typhoid in 1864, and shortly thereafter, her baby and husband died as well.

Mary married Alfred Pell in 1877.

Fanny married J. Pierpont Morgan in 1865, and in 1875 she introduced him to Mount Desert Island, reviving her delight in the island. They stayed at Rodick's Hotel in Bar Harbor and went for a picnic to Great Head and Sand Beach. Whether or not their nine-year-old daughter, Louisa, accompanied them on this trip is not clear from the account in Morgan's biography, but it was Herbert Satterlee, Morgan's biographer and Louisa's husband, who built a prefabricated house and Beatrix Farrand garden on Great Head, a wedding present to the couple from Morgan.

Clara married Frederick Street Hoppin in 1865.

Charlie married Helen McLeod Dawson in 1878; and later in 1886, Jennie Bigelow, a neighbor nearby on the Hudson River. He became a partner in his father's law firm. It was his descendants who preserved the F.E. Church sketches and drawings, later found in a box among his father's papers.

Julia married Francis G. Brown.

[Louisa "Daisy" Kirkland Tracy, the Tracy's last child, was not born until 1859, well after the Mount Desert trip.]

The Fay Family

Harrison Fay came from a Southboro, Mass. family, and he and his wife, **Sarah**, lived the remainder of their lives at 43 Linden Street in Brookline, Mass. He was a successful merchant on Commercial St., Boston. None of his sons married, and one son and daughter continued to live at home. His eldest daughter, Cornelia, was the only one to marry and have children. The Fays experienced a devastating year in 1869 when Cornelia died after the birth of her third child, their second son died at sea, and their three grandchildren were taken from them by their son-in-law and sent to the care of a convent. These staunch Episcopalians were never able to forgive their son-in-law, James Kent Stone, for the loss of their grandchildren as a direct result of his horrifying (to them) conversion to Catholicism. Yet, after Harrison Fay's death, Kent wrote his old friend, Jim Fay, in an attempt to comfort him, remembering Jim's father's character as "so hallowed and so gracious." [2] There is a plaque in Harrison Fay's memory at St. Paul's Church, Brookline, which reads, "Rejoicing in hope, patient in tribulation."

Cornelia "Cornie" Fay, the "Miss Fay" of the diary account, was senior by five years to James Kent Stone, a lively fifteen-year-old youth in the diary, whom she was to marry in 1863. They spent an idyllic summer in Campton, N.H., several years after the Maine trip, where he wrote a long (and lovely) religious poem inspired by their time together.[3] By all accounts, Cornelia Fay was highly regarded by her peers and much loved by both the Fay and Stone families. Not only was she an accomplished musician, but she had a pleasing personality. From her many well-written and informative letters to friends,[4] we glimpse her nature and understand why her young husband was so grief-stricken by her death, which triggered his final conversion to the Catholic faith, and led to the ultimate abandonment of his two surviving daughters.

James H. Fay was James Kent Stone's best friend in Brookline, although two years his senior. They both attended Mr. Dixwell's private school, and overlapped at Harvard College for at least a year. Jim Fay went on to Harvard Law School, but spent the better part of his working life in New York City where he practiced the legal profession. After the death of his sister, Cornelia, her husband Kent's conversion, and the loss of his two nieces to the convent, he sought (unsuccessfully) to have his old friend, Kent, committed as insane. Like his parents, he remained unforgiving. He never married, but was a dutiful son, returning home to Brookline each weekend to be with his widowed mother. After retirement, he lived out his remaining years in the Linden Street family home, caring for his invalid sister, Fanny. A founder of the Harvard Club of New York, where his portrait still hangs, he was also active in the Brookline Historical Society. Both groups wrote tributes to him after his death. In his last years, he made a gesture to his nieces, living then in California, by sending them their mother Cornelia's papers, letters and photographs.[5] In his will, he left his sizeable estate to St. Paul's Church and the Massachusetts General Hospital, with small bequests to loyal servants.

Arthur K. Fay, the second son, died in the same year as his sister, Cornie, and was buried at sea in the Indian Ocean.

Clement K. Fay, the third son, also attended Harvard and its Law School. He practiced law in Boston, never married, and lived at home with his parents and sister in Brookline. After the death of his sister, Cornelia, he was music and choir director of St. Paul's Church for many years, composing music for the choir as well. Known as a person of "settled convictions," he served in the Massachusetts Legislature for two terms as an Independent, as State Prison Commissioner for one year, and as President of the Society of Colonial Wars for a period of time.

Frances "Fanny" Fay, the youngest daughter, never married, and lived at home. Cornie and Kent's youngest daughter was named for her.

***

Frederic Edwin Church was born in Hartford, Connecticut, a descendant of Richard Church, an original "proprietor" of Hartford in the 17th century. He was a painter of great distinction in the Hudson River School. His formal study had been minimal, although his last two years (1844 - 46) with Thomas Cole, in Cole's home in Catskill on the Hudson River, later influenced him to design and build his own home, *Olana*, in nearby Hudson, New York. Olana, an exotic Moorish creation whose style was inspired by his trips to the Middle East, is now a museum. Only two years after the visit to Somesville with the Tracy party, he was to paint the first of his two most famous paintings, *Niagara*, and two years after that, the other, *Heart of the Andes*. Church's theory of art, he often said, was "no theory." "More precisely," he said, "I believe the artist should paint what he sees."[6] In 1860, he married Isabella Mortimer Carnes, daughter of Francis Carnes, the U.S. Naval Attaché in Paris. The sudden death of his two oldest children of diptheria before age three was a lasting sorrow for Church, although later he had four more children, naming one for his great friend, Theodore Winthrop.

***

Theodore Winthrop, a descendant of the Massachusetts Winthrops, was a poet in his college years at Yale, and later a budding novelist. He died gallantly in 1861, the first casualty of the first major engagement of the Civil War at Great Bethel (between Hampton and Yorktown, Virginia). He was eulogized in an elaborate burial ceremony at Yale. After the 1855 Mount Desert visit, Winthrop accompanied Church on a wilderness trip to Katahdin in 1856. He described the trip in an article, "Life in the Open Air," in *Atlantic Monthly*, not published until after his death in 1862. His first published work, in 1859, was a pamphlet to accompany Church's famous painting, *The Heart of the Andes*. All his other writings and novels appeared posthumously, and made him famous for a half-century afterwards. *Mr. Waddy's Return*, an early work but his last novel, published in 1904, has a chapter set on Mount Desert around Schooner Head, and derives directly from his visit there with the Tracy party.[7] He also wrote a long narrative poem called *The Camp* about getting lost on Western Mountain, an incident in the diary. (See note 30 in the *Log Book* section of Notes & Sources for a fragment of the poem.)

The Stone Family

Rev. John S. Stone, during his long and successful career, served as rector of a number of churches from Philadelphia to Boston. He was later to become the first Dean and professor of Systematic Divinity at the Episcopal Theological School in Cambridge, Mass. During his lifetime, he wrote several important books on religious subjects. He was guide and pastor to Phillips Brooks and his family. In all his posts, he enjoyed wide support from wealthy and prominent lay people up and down the East coast. His first wife was Sophie Morrison Adams and they had five children, only two of whom, Archibald and Mary, survived. (Archibald took the name of Morrison for inheritance reasons. He too was ordained and taught at Kenyon College, where he saw much of his half-brother, Kent and his wife, Cornie). Rev. Stone later married Mary Kent with whom he had six children: James Kent, William, Henry Van Dyke, Elizabeth (Bessie), Charles, and Philip. By all accounts, his attitude at the time of his son Kent's conversion was exemplary. In a long letter to Kent, he was both accepting and respectful of his son's decision.

One senses that his reasonable nature ultimately prevailed, (for example, his talk with Tracy in the diary on the subject of Catholicism) in spite of anti-Catholic rhetoric from time-to-time in his sermons.[8]

Mary Kent Stone, second wife of the Rev. Stone, was deeply attached to her eldest son, Kent, as revealed through their frequent correspondence,[9] even while she expressed despair over her son's conversion to the Catholic faith. Kent had hopes that she too would eventually see the light and convert to the true church. More than her husband, it was difficult for her to reconcile herself to Kent's conversion, but eventually, she re-established a bridge of understanding between them. In addition, she was courageous in accepting Kent's decision to have her two surviving granddaughters adopted into a Catholic family — saying at the time 'their new mother would be like a daughter to her.' She also made an effort to go to Philadelphia and meet the little girls' new mother at the time of the adoption, which Kent had asked her to do and to give her approval.[10]

Kent Stone's life story was to unfold with tragic effect to many people on the trip. Kent showed exceptional promise as a youth, and had the twin endowments of good looks and intelligence. After Harvard, he traveled on the Continent for a year, fought in the Civil War, was ordained in the Episcopal Church, married Cornelia Fay, sister of his friend James Fay, served as presidents of both Kenyon and Hobart Colleges, and fathered two daughters before a series of events changed the course of all their lives. In the same year, 1869, his wife died following the birth of their third child, and Kent converted to Catholicism and entered a monastic order, shocking both his wife's family and his own... all this coming rapidly upon his departure from Kenyon College to the Presidency of Hobart College, the result of a bitter theological controversy which was to irrevocably affect the course of Kenyon's history.

Although Kent gravitated more and more toward High Church Episcopal philosophy in his thinking while at Kenyon, it took a visionary dream not long before his wife died, and the crisis and grief over her death, to catalyze his decision to convert. The decision appeared to many to be sudden, when in fact, some observant friends saw it brewing. The theological controversy in which he was embroiled at Kenyon while President (high church vs. low church) revealed his change of direction, a steady progression toward Roman Catholic doctrine. Given that Kent's father was much-admired as an individual, eminent in Episcopal circles, and a leader of the Evangelical movement (low church), it was perhaps especially difficult for his son, Kent, an equally talented and ambitious individual, to carve out territory that he could call his own.

Not long after his wife's death, Kent took his three young daughters away from their Fay grandmother, and put them in the care of the convent of the Sisters of Mercy in Manchester, New Hampshire. At the same time, he added to their given names of Cornelia and Ethel the name Mary, and at last found a name for the new baby, Mary Frances. While at the convent, Mary Ethel died of pneumonia. He then removed the oldest girl, Mary Cornelia, and the baby, Mary Frances, from the convent and sent them to a childless California couple for adoption, unintentionally severing almost all contact with them for some years. It was during this period that his former friend, James Fay, tried to have him declared insane.

Kent had entered the Paulist monastic order in New York state. Until the adoption of his daughters around 1872, however, he was unable to pursue his true wishes to become a monk in the Passionist Order in Ohio, where he finally took the name "Fidelis of the Cross." The Passionist Order was an austere order. The Order's chief purpose was "the giving of missions to the people, and retreats to the clergy and religious communities." Their work involved extensive travel to foreign countries, which was to be the pattern of the remaining fory-nine years of Kent's life.[11] As he had throughout his early life, he distinguished himself in his new calling, both in service and the written word. His most important work was *An Invitation Heeded*, laying forth the arguments between Catholic and Protestant.

Several accounts have been written of his life and conversion, including his autobiographical one, *An Awakening and What Followed.* It was not until the end of his life that he was able to re-establish contact with his daughters, now called by their new family names, Mary and

Frances O'Connor, living in California. Their new mother at the time of the adoption had insisted that he relinquish almost total contact with his daughters, pleading that it would be better for them. It was the prevailing opinion at the time that children soon forgot and that it was wiser if there was no conflict about whom a child should love. (Consider however that at the time, the eldest daughter Mary Cornelia, who was age eight and her father's favorite, had lost over a three-year period her mother, her sister and closest companion Ethel, her grandmother's care, her father's love and presence, and three familiar homes). Kent himself had never intended to sever all contact with his children, a loss which he grieved for the next forty-nine years and an unexpected burden on the "Cross" of his chosen name.[12]

Late in Kent's life, his autobiographical account, *An Awakening*, was read by his youngest daughter, Frances, and a real, if brief, relationship with his children was re-established. In his eighties, and seriously ill, Kent made the long journey to California in Frances' care. His adored eldest daughter, now called Mary, was the widow of Charles de Cazeotte, and the mother of a grown son, Michael. Kent was delighted to meet and come to know his grandson, and although he and Mary had grown spiritually and emotionally apart, it was Frances whom he never really knew with whom he now established a bond.[13] In the sixth month of his visit, his health suddenly deteriorated, and he died in Frances' arms.

The abrupt turn in Kent's thinking and career had its rational and intellectual component, but no doubt, there was also an emotional component, less obvious but influential. The following facts, from what little is known, are suggestive of what that might have been. One, Kent was deeply attached to his mother. Two, his wife was five years his senior, and the older sister of his best friend. Three, he never seemed to consider taking personal responsibility for his three children after their mother's death. All three seem to imply unusual dependency, and perhaps also a feeling of inadequacy. The perception that monastic life offers a kind of perpetual care, as well as harmony of thought and purpose, may have been the decisive factor in his becoming a monk.

William "Willie" Stone is the recipient of a letter from his elder brother, Kent, which can be found reprinted under Notes.[14] It was written at the time of the trip to Somesville and sent to Willie after he and his younger brother, Hal, returned home to Brookline with their parents. Kent tantalizes Willie with a partial account of getting lost in the "wilderness" and boasts of his exploits while fishing. Kent also has a few words for his brother Hal and his sister, Bessie, as well. The only thing known about Willie's later life is a letter written by the Rev. Stone asking a friend to help his son, Willie, find employment.[15]

Henry "Hal" Stone was killed in the Civil War in the Battle of Gettysburg. He died in a gallant but misguided attack with the Massachusetts 5th Regiment, which later turned out to be the result of an incorrect battle order.[16] It was Kent's task to go to the battlefield by lantern light to recover his brother's body.

Notes and Sources

Foreword

1. Agassiz, Elizabeth Clary, *Louis Agassiz: His Life and Correspondence*, 2 vols., Houghton & Mifflin & Co., Boston, MA, 1886, vol. II, pp. 622 - 23.
   Drake, Samuel Adams, *Nooks and Corners of the New England Coast*, Harper, New York, N.Y., 1875, pp. 42 & 48.
2. The envelope in which the copy of the diary was presented to Jesup Library had "U.S. Department of the Interior, National Park Service, Acadia National Park, Bar Harbor, Me." printed on the outside. Underneath was stamped, "official business," and in pencil below that, "G.B. Dorr." At the time, Dorr was Director of the Park. Below that it said, "Tracy Diary, Reviewed Feb. 3, 1940, P.L.S." (the initials of George Dorr's secretary. See *Acadia National Park, George B. Dorr's Triumph...*, by Sargent F. Collier, 1965, Knowlton & McCleary, Farmington, Maine).
3. August 13 in the diary, in Tracy's continuing diatribe against the Catholic Church, note the final phrase, "yet is the synagogue of Satan."
4. Lambruschini, Cardinal Luigi, *A Polemical Treatise on the Immaculate Conception of the Blessed Virgin*, written in 1842, published 1855 by D.& J. Sadlier & Co., Boston, MA, translation of the French by Mrs. J. Sadlier, and the Latin by a clergyman. The volume also includes *A History of the Doctrine* by Father Felix, S.J., and learned appendices including The Declaration by Pope Pius IX, Dec. 8, 1854:

   "That it is the dogma of faith that the Blessed Virgin Mary, from the first instant of her conception, by a privilege and special grace of God in virtue of the merits of Jesus Christ, Sorrow of Mankind, was preserved intact from every stain of original sin."
5. Smith, Walter George and Helen Grace, *Fidelis of the Cross, James Kent Stone*, G.P. Putnam's Sons, The Knickerbocker Press, New York, N.Y., 1926.

Page 173 — quotation from *The Invitation Heeded*, a book by J.K. Stone:

"...opinions imbibed from infancy through every pore and never counteracted. If these opinions were prejudices, how almost impossible would it be for truth to penetrate them! I thought of the English language in which I had learned to think and to impress my thoughts; and I remembered how for three hundred years that tongue had been one vast engine of ceaseless attack upon the Roman Catholic Church; how its literature was saturated with a spirit of deadly antagonism to that Church, not in the department of theology only but of history and poetry and travels and fiction, aye! and the very primers in the hands of the little children."

Page 159 - 60 —

"Had he [JKS] taken the opposite course, and, and served [severed] from the via media of Anglicanism into frank Agnosticism, it may be believed that many of his former brethren would have accepted the change without so deep a disgust; but to become a Catholic was almost repugnant as to decency."

6. Richardson, Robert D., Jr., *The Mind on Fire*, University of California Press, 1995, p. 44.
7. In Jesup Memorial Library, Bar Harbor, with copy of the Diary.
8. From the Diary: "Noisily contending for the due liberation of three millions of negroes, they assail the union which defends the liberties of seven times three millions of caucasians...." (July 31). "...efficient instrumentality of the Ethiopian Minstrelsy" (Sept. 3).
9. Agassiz, *Louis Agassiz...*, ibid.

   Drake, *Nooks and Corners...*, ibid.
10. Morison, Samuel Eliot, *The Story of Mount Desert Island*, Atlantic Monthly Press, Little, Brown & Co., Boston, MA, 1960, p. 9 — from Champlain account of naming of the island.
11. Information provided by Mrs. Martin Roberts, wife of a descendant of Tobias Roberts, via Geraldine Sweet, Northeast Harbor.
12. Sanderson, Virginia Somes, *The Living Past*, Beech Hill Publishing, Mount Desert, Maine, 1982, p. 149.
13. Joy, Adelma Somes, unpublished memoir, in the archives of the Mt. Desert Island Historical Society, Somesville, Maine:

    The following memoir, one of several written by Adelma Somes Joy, daughter of Jacob Somes and great-granddaughter of Abraham Somes, the first settler of Mt. Desert, was recorded later in her life and therefore inaccurate in some particulars, such as the year the Charles Tracy party visited Somesville. However, much is well-remembered and contributes significant detail to our knowledge of the time. The spelling and punctuation are her own. Most insertions may have been made by her niece, Mrs. V.S. Sanderson.

Reminiscence of Somesville

Somewhere about 1853 or '54, [Fredric] Church the artist came to Bar Harbor and put on canvass the beautiful mountain and ocean scenery of Mt. Desert Island. Wether his pictures drew attention to its beauties or not from that time we began to have what we now call summer guests. In the summer of 1854, the artist Church came with quite a party to Somesville that being the only place on the Island [at that time] that could acomadate so many. The little Tavern Mr. Daniel Somes Landlord was filled and many lodged out. It was a very pleasant summer and they seemed to enjoy it very much going on picnics to the different places, climbing mountains, sailing, but mostly to Bar Harbor. At that time I do not think there was any place in Bar Harbor where one could get board or lodging and I think the artist stayed with the Lynams at Schooner Head. To us younger people of Somesville at that date Bar Harbor was almost unknown. We knew master Stephen Higgins, a master builder of vessels launched from our shipyards and that he lived in Bar Harbor. About all we knew of Hulls Cove was that master Brewer and Capt. Richard Higgins came from that place but all other places in Eden we knew well and most everybody living there. But to return to our summer guests of 1854. If they enjoyed their summer, we resident people certainly enjoyed seeing them. One of the young ladies we saw more of as she seldom went on the excursions with the others but prefered strolling around the ponds and brooks in the village with a little sister [Annie Tracy and Julia Tracy]. The ponds were much prettier then than now. Water plants with pretty blossoms; some yellow, some white. The running brooks were red with cardinals, but there are hardly any left now. At the close of the season, the little village was all excitement as invitations had been sent to every family from the summer party to a reception at the little Tavern. We of course dressed in our best, and I will say here that high necked dresses and long sleeves had just come in style; and I cannot remember of seeing a low neck or short sleeve that evening. Dotted muslin fan waists and silk skirts predominated. After removing our wraps we were ushered into the parlor and introduced to Mr. Lynam and wife and daughter, they being the guests of honor. We younger people soon left for the dining room which had been cleared for dancing, and to the music of one violin [a flute is also mentioned in *The Log Book*] we probably enjoyed ourselves as well as the generation of today with their orchestra of several instruments. You will wonder how we learned to dance in those early days with no Halls. In the second story of the wool factory was the carding machine which took up a very small place acrost one end. All the rest of the room was for bundles of wool to be carded and I have seen it full as it could be crowded into only a narrow aisle to walk through. In winter there was no wool there and it was scrubbed and scoured and waxed and the carding machine partioned off so we had a very large hall and a very large dancing class. So that evening at the party we could waltz. Polka and Shotiche [schottische — a round dance in duple measure resembling a slow polka] and dance quadrilles as well as all contra dances. The dances of today are not the same. This is the incident that has sent my memory wandering back to that long ago summer. In the present year of 1918 Aug. the 15th at the sale in the Library building in Somesville two ladies of that Aug. party of 1854 were present. One of the summer guests [Mrs. J.P. Morgan who expressed a wish to meet with someone from the village who had been at that party] and one of the resident people [Mrs. A.F. Joy] but they missed seeing each other. The resident one is all there is left with one exception to remember. Just two left in Mt. Desert that waltzed and danced to the music of that one violin and perhaps the summer guest was all that is left of that happy party. The waters of Somes Sound dance and sparkle in the sunshine today just as they did in that long ago: the ponds are just as still and the brooks babble over their rocky beds and the appearance of the village is very little changed; but the change is that the older generation has passed away and another generation is passing away and the younger ones are filling the places. The resident woman as she sat outside the library and looked at the scene so familiar to her felt an inexpressible sadness. Seemed as though she had nothing left but the memory of those she had lost.

Such is life.

Northeast Harbor, Aug. 19th 1918
Adelma F. Somes Joy (1838 — 1930)

Members of the Party

The Tracy Family

Satterlee, Herbert L., *J. Pierpont Morgan, An Intimate Portrait*, The Macmillan Co., New York, N.Y., 1939.

Tracy Genealogical Chart and Reminiscences, and *The Kirkland Family*, by V.C. Sanborn, Press of David Clapp & Son, Boston, MA, 1894, and from letters to Mrs. Charles Tracy from her husband and daughter, Annie. Courtesy of Anne Eristoff.

Joy, *Memoir....*

The Fay Family

Brookline Historical Society Proceedings, 1915 - 20, published by the Society.

Brookline, Jamaica Plain and West Roxbury Directory of 1871, published by Dean Dudley & Co., Boston, MA, 1871.

Tax List for 1860, Brookline, from Brookline, MA Reports, 1861 - 1870.

The Boston Directory, published by George Adams, 1857.

Harvard Directory of Graduates, Harvard University, Cambridge, MA.

Harvard University Alumni Records, obituaries of James H. Fay, class of 1859, and Clement K. Fay, class of 1867, and memoir of James H. Fay by Winthrop S. Scudder, presented to the Harvard Club of New York.

Smith, *Fidelis....*

Amory, Robert, *My Journey of 1857*, unpublished memoir, courtesy of Gertrude McCue.

The Church Family

Huntington, David C., *The Landscapes of Frederic Edwin Church, Vision of an American Era*, George Braziller, New York, N.Y., 1966.

Carr, Gerald L., *Frederic Edwin Church: Catalogue Raisonné of Works of Art at Olana State Historic Site*, 2 volumes, Text and Plates, Cambridge University Press, 1994.

Warner, Charles Dudley, unfinished and unpublished biography of F.E. Church, at Olana State Historic Site, Hudson, N.Y.

Theodore Winthrop

Winthrop, Theodore, *Introduction to John Brent*, first published by Ticknor and Fields, Boston, MA, 1862, reissued 1970 by College & University Press, New Haven, CT., with a new introduction by H. Dean Propst.

Huntington, *The Landscapes...*

The Stone Family

Smith, *Fidelis...*

Library of Congress Art Reference

Burton, Katherine, *No Shadow of Turning: The Life of James Kent Stone (Father Fidelis of the Cross)*, Longmans, Green & Co., 1944.

Episcopal Diocese of Massachusetts, Boston, MA.

Letter to Willie from James Kent Stone, published in *Fidelis of the Cross*, see note 14 of Afterword section for full text.

Packard, Joseph, *Recollections of a Long Life*, Episcopal Review, date unknown, available in the archives of Episcopal Divinity School, Cambridge, MA.

Muller, James Arthur, *The Episcopal Theological School, 1867 - 1943*, published by the Episcopal Theological School, Cambridge, MA, 1943.

Blackman, George L., *Faith and Freedom, A Study of Theological Education and the Episcopal Theological School*, The Seabury Press, 1967.

Lawrence, William, *73 Years of the Episcopal Theological School: A Narrative*, 1940, Episcopal Divinity School Archives, Cambridge, MA.

Malone, Dumas, *The Dictionary of American Biography*, Volume 9, Charles Scribner & Sons, New York, N.Y., p. 79.

World Book Encyclopedia, 1994, by World Book, Inc. Entry on James Kent (1763 - 1847): Chief Justice of the Supreme Court of New York, 1804; Chancellor of New York Court of Chancery, 1814 - 1823; author of *Commentaries on American Law* (1826-30), which had great influence on American legal practice.

Robert S. Littell

Huntington, *The Landscapes...*

The Boston Directory...

Littell's Living Age, weekly periodical, Littell, Son & Co., Boston, MA., archives of the Brookline Public Library.

History of St. Paul's Church, Brookline, Church Library, Brookline, MA., 1949.

The Titus Family

Olana State Historic Site archives; letters from a Mr. J. B. Titus to F. E. Church and from Mrs. L. A. Titus to Mrs. Church, 1863 (or 1864).

The Log Book

1. Pavement
2. Point off of Rhode Island.
3. Mill town, Buzzards Bay, Mass. Leading textile manufacturing city, particularly in cottons.
4. Well-known hotel of the period.
5. This very large painting on stage in Faneuil Hall, by George P.A. Healey (1813-1894), depicts Daniel Webster, Senator from Massachusetts, on January 25, 1830, defending New England against attack from a Southerner, Senator Hayne of South

Carolina, before leading politicians of the day in the Senate, and prominent members of Washington society in the audience. The painting had been commissioned by King Louis Phillipe of France, who died before it was completed in 1848. In 1851, it was purchased by a wealthy Bostonian, who presented it to the city. [Therefore, when Charles Tracy viewed the painting in 1855, it was relatively unknown.] Information from *Blue Guide of Boston and Cambridge*, 1984; courtesy of Art Department, Boston Public Library.

6. Tracy's designation for someone odd, or colorful.
7. Compare with departure, pages 136 and 137.
8. The first steamboat to Southwest Harbor, then part of the Town of Tremont. It was owned by the Eastern Steamboat Co., for whom Deacon H.H. Clark was the agent. Clark also built the steamboat wharf where the passengers landed. (Thornton, Mrs. Seth S., *Traditions and Records of Southwest Harbor and Somesville, Mount Desert Island, Maine*, 1938, p. 170 - 172).
9. ibid., Clark Tavern owned by Deacon H.H. Clark, p. 174.
10. In 1846, a Prohibition law was enacted in Maine, and in 1849, severe punishments for lawbreakers were added. From *Maine, A History*, 1974 facsimile of 1919 edition, edited by Louis Clinton Hatch, New Hampshire Publishing Co., Somersworth, NH, pp. 296 - 302.
11. Actually Butter Hill then, now Storm King, near West Point on Hudson River.
12. Tracy's invention.
13. Great Long Pond.
14. Correct attire (including long skirts) was expected, an obstacle to strenuous activity on hot days.
15. Mason Point.
16. The practice of singing psalms during worship.
17. Somersault; 'somerset' still acceptable.
18. Mrs. Rhoda Wasgatt Richardson (1807 - 1877 or 79). The house remains in the Richardson family today.
19. Newburgh, N.Y., on the Hudson River.
20. Probably Round Pond.
21. Most likely a church off the Seal Cove Road near the Cape Road intersection, in what was then known as the town of Center. See *Bar Harbor Times*, Section B, p. 2, October 8, 1992.
22. Now Adam's Island

23. Tracy spelling; actual spelling 'Katahdin,' an Abnaki Indian word meaning 'principal mountain.' The Indians believed a spirit inhabited each mountain and Katahdin was the name of this particular spirit. (Rutherford, Philip R., *Dictionary of Maine Place Names*, 1970).

24. Here, probably means blueberry; sometimes also huckleberry (or hurtleberry).

25. Gymnastics.

26. Archaic, meaning named or called.

27. Fishing boats, generally gaff-rigged mackerel fishing boats in those days.

28. Above the farmhouse of William Lynam (1795-1857) and wife, Hannah (died 1851; most likely his first wife, and mother of his children). Gravestones in old Schooner Head Graveyard. Charles William and Nancy Jane are also members of the Lynam family (see diary entries, Wednesday, Aug. 15 and Friday, Aug. 24).

29. Upper Hadlock Pond.

30. Sargent, Parkman and Penobscot Mountains.

31. See Foreword for explanation, page 20.

32. George Huntington (1770 - 1842), brother of Rachel Huntington, Charles Tracy's mother. From *The Huntington Family in This Country*, by Rev. E.B. Huntington, Stamford, CT., 1863. George was the first Huntington to move from the family home in Norwich, CT. to New York state. He came to be called the "Patriarch of the Village" of Rome, N.Y., where he lived. He was a successful businessman known for "sagacity, probity, and fair dealing." (D.C. Huntington, author of *The Landscapes of Frederic Edwin Church*, cited in this book as a source, is also a distant relative.)

33. Worship of the Virgin Mary.

34. Sargent Pond, a favorite spot for a quick dip after a hot climb.

35. Church has a pencil drawing of a fleet estimated at one hundred stretched out on the horizon. (1850, File box 124, Cooper Hewitt Museum.)

36. Mt. Desert Rock Lighthouse built in 1847.

37. Actually 19 sketches.

38. Of horses.

39. Champlain Mountain.

40. Excellent description of dramatic feature on Schooner Head. Also see note 14 of Afterword, *Letter to Willie*.

41. Bernard Mountain, or Western Mountain itself.

42. The following is the surprising, and somewhat less accurate account of the whole

adventure from Drake, *Nooks and Corners...*, "...Church...did not always come for work. On one occasion, as leader of a merry party, he was lost on Beech Mountain, and passed the night there. With rare pre-vision he had provided an axe, with plenty of robes and wraps. At the foot of the mountain, the carriage was sent back to the village. Church was too good a woodman not to use his axe to make a shanty of boughs, while the robes, when spread upon fragrant heaps of spruce, made excellent couches for the laughing girls that were in his protection. Meanwhile consternation reigned at Somesville...until the next morning, when they entered the village as if nothing unusual had happened." [Thus is history made.] See also, Kent's letter to Willie, note 14 in Afterword.

Below is another rendering of the adventure taken from a long poem by Theodore Winthrop, *The Camp, An Idyl given in XI Filtes*, from the David Huntington Archives of Olana State Historic Site:

Kent's Commentaries

[*note: this is a play on the title of Kent's grandfather's book.*]

Sleeping he woke
Eyes fully filled with smoke,
Puzzled and blinking. —
(He ____; Kent Stone speaks)
"Can a dream
Be real as this? Could I have gone to bed
Booted and panted? Oh! methinks my head
Has been log-pillowed. I must scream
For I am stiff-necked, Hallo! Trees!
They've left the windows up. Some breeze
Has dewy showered me. Is that ceiling sky?
No starry bits of whitewash lime my eye.
This is no house — or if house 'tis all door
Whence comes the smoke? it seems to pour
As if my eyes were chimney holes.
Why there's the fire! They'll burn the floor those coals!
Where my wash basin stood, a lake
Is pitcher, basin, mirror all in one —
My sleep was sound, and soundless. Did I take
An impish midnight stroll here all alone?
T'was a hard spot I chose — Kent on Blackstone!
My commentaries on my sheets are brief,
They are dry leaves...

43. Another form of 'stayed' — *The Concise Oxford Dictionary,* 6th edition, Oxford

University Press, 1976.

44. Sometimes referred to as Devil's Den, today known as Anemone Cave.

45. Great Head.

46. Another Catholic writer.

47. A total of seven guests (and a nurse) who leave the day before the party.

48. St. Sauveur.

49. Farmhouse where boats for Eagle Lake are rented out (see also Friday, Aug. 10 in diary).

50. See notes 11, 12 and 13 of Foreword.

51. Secretion from the head of sperm whales used for cosmetics and candles.

52. An unaccompanied part song scored for three or more male voices that was popular in the 18th century. —*American Heritage Dictionary*, 3rd edition, Houghton Mifflin, 1992.

53. Theodore Winthrop's sister, Laura Winthrop Johnson, wrote an account of decorations made by Church for this affair in a memoir of her brother after his death. (Courtesy of Gerald Carr.)

54. Irene and Iqua; see Foreword, note 11.

55. Traveling rug — *The Concise Oxford Dictionary...*

56. See Joy, *Reminiscence...*, Foreword, note 13.

57. Jordan Pond and The Bubbles.

58. Between Champlain and Dorr Mountains.

59. The Old Bar Harbor Road then via the Knox Road to Somesville, perhaps.

60. He may have intended to say 'Clark's' here.

Afterword

1. Joy, *Memoir...*

2. Smith, *Fidelis....*, p. 285.

3. ibid., p. 84 - 86.

4. ibid.

5. Burton, *No Shadow of Turning...*,

6. Huntington, *The Landscapes...*, p. 29.

7. Winthrop, Theodore, *Mr. Waddy's Return*, Henry Holt and Co., New York, N.Y.,

1904, edited by Burton E. Stevenson. Schooner Head descriptive passage from the book follows:

"When the rustling of her passage through the thicket ceased, she could hear the neighbour crashing of breakers. Black Rock Head rose to the north of the rocky cove, home of Dempster's boat. Southward, stood other headlands, and southernmost, Wrecker's Point, where all the fury of surges driven by the southeast gale would be felt. When the mingled mist, spray, and rain drifted away for a moment, and shrank to give space to a great, howling blast, she could see a lofty white ghostly object, like a ship in full sail, dimly visible, suddenly lift itself against the dark front of the head. Then it sank away, dashed to nothingness of foamy wreck. A hollow roar came, as the cavernous cleft of the Head was overcrowded with the breaker, and, gushing up, the mass of uprising waters overwhelmed the promontory and, spreading, mantled over its smooth surfaces and tore in many cataracts down its chasms to the sea. The Head, through veils of mist, seemed like a distant dome mountain of snow."

8. Smith, *Fidelis...*, p. 5. Quoted is Miss Charlotte Dana, who heard him "eloquently argue" at St. Paul's Church the following, "The Catholic Church is so strong today, and it has triumphed over so much in the course of history — not only the external opposition, but more still, corruption from within — that it simply cannot be of human origin. It must therefore be the work of the devil." This does not sound like the man who calmed Tracy with good sense and spiritual wisdom on August 13 in the diary account.

9. ibid, Chapters I - V.

10. ibid., p. 238-39.

11. ibid., p. 247.

12. ibid., p. 235. "As time went on, their [Mr. and Mrs. Michael J. O'Connor] relations ceased with his [JKS'] mother and the maternal relatives of the children. As they passed on from childhood, they were given every advantage of education and travel, but their father's name and his people were for them practically non-existent.

    Here was a tragedy which might easily been averted. Try as he would the image of those baby faces was stamped on his heart..."

13. ibid., p. 420, from a letter to his daughter Frances near the end of his life:

    "...In all my life I have had four great loves: My mother; my sister, Bessie; your mother, — and your sister, Mary Cornelia. And I think the last was the greatest. Hers was the name which I wrote upon the sand, and which the waves washed out. It was not of her mother I was thinking. And I used to fancy that some day

I might publish the verses in a book, and that at last some day, when I should be long gone, and almost forgotten, she might come across the book, and might light upon the verses, and wonder whose the name could have been, and might come to the conclusion that it was probably her mother's — and she would be mistaken. Some day, if I live and gain a little strength, I may write out for you some little memories of her sweet babyhood and childhood which will show you how and why I loved her so dearly.

And you, my daughter, how is it that after all these long years...you who have been by me so long unnoticed, almost unperceived, should suddenly without warning take the place in my poor heart which no one had ever really filled?..."

14. ibid., pps. 10 - 11, Kent Stone's letter to his brother, Willie, who returned home to Brookline before Kent in 1855:

Your room, Church Colony
Monday afternoon, August 20th

Dear Willie,

What a time I have had since you left Somesville! Although it is not quite a week, yet I have done so many things in that time that it seems very much longer, & I begin to feel quite lonely & homesick. You went mackerel fishing once while you were here & caught nothing, did you not? Well, in the same place, the other side of Bar Island, a party of us went fishing soon after you left, and caught 40 mackerel. Almost every day since then a party of us has gone out and caught on an average about *one hundred* mackerel. It is rare sport, & we have totally given up fishing for flounders & Tommy Cod. We have also caught some Haike, Polluk & Smelts. I have caught more fish than any other one in the party so far, generally catching half of the fish caught by all.

The other day we all rode over to "Schooner Head," where we saw one of the greatest curiosities I have ever seen or ever expect to see — A very wonderful & gigantic cave among the rocks, on the sea shore. You look down a perpendicular chasm, about 75 ft. deep, the same in length, & about a yard & a half in width, & see below a nice, flat, rock bottom. Presently to the great surprise of all, you see "Mr. Church" step out, as if from the rocks and walk along the bottom. The mystery is soon unraveled. There is a "cylindrical," (a pretty long word) passage about ten feet in diameter, & twenty in length, leading from the inside on the bottom, to the open air, on the seashore. Soon after we all descended on the outside & went through the passage into the wonderful cave. It is well worth coming up to Mt. Desert to see.

But the great thing is coming. — Something which I can talk about all the rest of my life. A party of us, myself included, set out on Saturday through unknown regions in the forest, to find a certain lake, & got overtaken by darkness, & had to "Camp out" all night by the shores of the lake. The story is too long & too interesting to be told with pen & ink, so you must wait patiently till next Wednesday, when I hope I shall be able to tell you with my lips. In the meantime, you must imagine all the particulars.

I am very glad to hear you are all so well in Brookline, especially Siddie. I am glad to hear my chickens come on so well, & it seems quite wonderful the progress little Smartie has made. Have they grown much larger? I sincerely hope Bully will come on well. Is he licked by any of the other young chickens? You have not told me which chicken you would like. If you want to write do it *right off*, for I leave here on Monday......Dear little Hal, you'll let me kiss you when I get home, won't you? Do you stick in a word or two next time Willie writes. I sleep in your bed now, all alone.

KENT

15. Correspondence of John Seeley Stone, Episcopal Divinity School, Cambridge, MA.

16. Smith, *Fidelis...*, pps. 87 - 88.